LIVING IN THE
Balance of
Grace and Faith

Combining Two Powerful Forces
to Receive from God

by
Andrew Wommack

Harrison House
Tulsa, Oklahoma

Unless otherwise indicated, all Scripture quotations are taken from the *King James Version* of the Bible.

The author has emphasized some words in Scripture quotations in italicized type.

Cover photo courtesy of Terry Moore, Family Studio.

12 11 10 09   10 9 8 7 6 5 4 3 2 1

Living in the Balance of Grace and Faith:
Combining Two Powerful Forces to Receive from God
ISBN 13: 978-1-57794-918-3
ISBN 10: 1-57794-918-8
Copyright © 2009 by Andrew Wommack Ministries, Inc.
P.O. Box 3333
Colorado Springs, Colorado 80934-3333
www.awmi.net

Published by Harrison House, LLC
P.O. Box 35035
Tulsa, Oklahoma 74153
www.harrisonhouse.com

Contents

Introduction

The balance of grace and faith is an important foundational truth. Whether you are consciously aware of it or not, you deal with this on a daily basis.

The body of Christ is basically divided into two groups: those who emphasize grace (God's part) and those who emphasize faith (our part).

One group preaches that everything is totally up to God. The other group teaches that there are many things that we must do. Both contend that the other group is totally wrong.

On a personal level, we may phrase this issue in many different ways, but it all comes down to the questions, "What part is God's responsibility, and what part is mine? What must I do?"

The Bible clearly teaches a balance between grace (God's part) and faith (our part). As you open up your heart to receive God's Word, the Lord has some life-changing truths He wants to share with you.

Chapter 1
Sodium and Chloride

We can become so familiar with a certain passage of scripture that we don't really know what it says. We don't pay attention to it anymore because it has become so common to us. Ephesians 2:8-9 has become one such passage for many believers.

For by grace are ye saved through faith; and that not of your-selves: it is the gift of God: Not of works, lest any man should boast.

There are some profound truths revealed here, one of which is that we are saved by grace through faith.

The body of Christ is basically divided into two groups: Those who emphasize grace (what God does) and those who emphasize faith (what we do).

One group preaches that everything is totally up to God. They say, "Everything is determined by the sovereignty of God. It's whatever He chooses." The other group teaches, "No, you have to do this and that, and this and that." Those who preach man's responsibility will normally say that those who teach that it's just all up to God are totally wrong. Those who preach that it's all up to God will teach against those who say man has some responsibility in the matter.

You might phrase this issue differently, but it all comes down to the question, "What do I do—what part is God's part, and what part is mine?" God's Word clearly teaches a balance between grace and faith.

Appeared to All Men

Even though the body of Christ typically divides into two camps—one emphasizing what God has to do, and the other emphasizing what we have to do—Ephesians 2:8-9 says that we are saved by grace through faith. We aren't saved by one or the other.

Now, to be technically correct, there is a parenthetical phrase in this passage in the last part of Ephesians 2:5, which says:

...by grace ye are saved.

I'm not arguing that it's wrong to say that we are saved by grace, but technically, it's not grace alone that saves us. It's really important that we understand this point. God has done so much for us by grace, but for us to receive what He has done there must be a positive response on our part, which is what the Bible calls "faith." There has to be a combination of both grace and faith.

You aren't saved by grace alone.

For the grace of God that bringeth salvation hath appeared to all men.

Titus 2:11

Grace is what God does for you. It's His part. It is something that was done for you before you existed. Grace has nothing to do with you. By definition, it is "unmerited, unearned, undeserved favor." If grace is something that God does and if grace alone saved, then every person would be saved because Titus 2:11 reveals that the grace of God that brings salvation has appeared to all men.

God's Grace

God's grace is the same towards everyone. God has been exactly the same toward every person who has ever lived. You may be wondering, *Then why did so-and-so get healed and I didn't? Why did God touch them and not me?* The problem is, you think that when you see something happen that God has done something or provided something for that person that He hasn't provided for you. God's grace is the same towards everybody because it's not based on, or tied to, what you do. God, by grace, has already brought salvation to every person on the face of this earth. (Titus 2:11.)

This is not something that is commonly understood. Most people believe that it's their performance that earns them extra pull and favor to get the power of God operating in their life. The truth is, the moment you begin relating God's blessing—the manifestation of His power in your life—to anything that you've done, then you have just voided grace. You've made God's blessing and manifestation in your life proportional to something that you've done. If you think that way, then you don't understand the grace of God.

God, by grace, already provided everything for you before you ever needed it. Take, for instance, salvation. Many people think that you have to ask God to forgive your sins and ask Jesus to come into your heart to receive salvation. They will pray, "Jesus, would You please come into my life?" They tell others "Just ask Christ to come into your life." That's not what salvation is.

A Nonissue

Acts 16:30-31 provides a scriptural example of someone receiving salvation. Paul and Silas were in the Philippian jail, and the jailer came to them and asked:

> *Sirs, what must I do to be saved?*
>
> Acts 16:30

They didn't answer by saying, "Ask Jesus to come into your life," or "Repent of your sins, and quit doing this and that." They simply responded:

> *Believe on the Lord Jesus Christ, and thou shalt be saved.*
>
> Acts 16:31

Believe what? This does not mean just believe that Jesus existed, or that He came.

Jesus didn't just die for the people He knew would accept Him someday.

He is the propitiation for our sins: and not for ours only, but also for the sins of the whole world.

1 John 2:2

Jesus died for every sinner who has ever lived on this earth. And He died for our sins two thousand years ago, long before we had ever committed them. The Lord doesn't wait until we ask Him, "Please come into my heart," to forgive us of our sins. The radical truth is, the sins of the entire world are already forgiven.

God forgave your sins before you existed. Before you were ever born, all of your sins were forgiven. Before you had ever committed a sin, God forgave them. Your sins are forgiven. Sin is actually a nonissue with God.

Already Been Forgiven

This is not the message of the Church today. The Church is basically preaching that every time you sin, it's an affront against God. They say, "You have to get that sin forgiven and under the blood before God can move in your life." That's not what the scriptures teach. The Word reveals that your sins are already forgiven. You don't have to ask God to forgive your sins or to come into your life. What you have to do is believe the Gospel—that Jesus has already come, He's already died and forgiven the sins of the world.

Someone might say, "Well then, if that's true, then everybody's saved, right?" No, this is not the case because grace alone doesn't save you. God, by grace, has made the provision and paid for every person's sins. People aren't going to go to hell for sexual immorality, murder, lying, or stealing. All of those sins have been paid for. The sin that is going to send people to hell is the singular sin of rejecting Jesus as their personal Savior. This is what the Bible reveals in John 16:

> When he [the Holy Spirit] is come, he will reprove the world of sin, and of righteousness, and of judgment.
>
> John 16:8

In verse 9 of this same chapter, Jesus explained that the sin the Holy Spirit would reprove the world of is the sin of not believing on Jesus.

> Of sin, because they believe not on me.
>
> John 16:9

The Church has been misrepresenting the Holy Spirit by saying that He's here to nail you every time you lie, cheat, and steal. That He'll get you every time you don't study the Word, or do this and not that. This preaching has made us sin-conscious. It has magnified sin. The truth is Jesus has already paid the price for all that. The Holy Spirit is only dealing with this one issue: Have you believed on the Lord Jesus Christ? If you have made Jesus your Lord, then all of your sins—past, present, and even future sins—have already been forgiven.

Identical Toward Us All

Preaching that truth would get me kicked out of most churches. That is why my citywide meetings are normally held in a neutral venue, like a hotel or conference center. There aren't very many churches that will let me share these truths because they're just so radical.

Sin has already been dealt with by grace. (Heb. 9, 10.) Because it has been dealt with by grace, that means it isn't dependent on whether you've asked Him to forgive you or not. The truth is, God provided salvation for the entire human race by grace.

Again, Titus 2:11 says:

> For the grace of God that bringeth salvation hath appeared to all men.

God's grace is extended exactly the same towards everybody—not only to you, but to every person on the face of the earth. Adolf Hitler had as much grace extended towards him as you and I have had extended towards us. Jesus loved every person who has done terrible things in the history of the world; He died for them and paid for their sins exactly the same as He did for all of the people who have received Him, love Him, and seek Him. The grace of God is identical toward us all.

Radical Truth

God, by grace, has already provided healing for everybody. One of my staff members who works at our citywide meetings used to be a quadriplegic. Now he's up walking around and doing great. He was supernaturally healed. Every quadriplegic has had the same exact grace extended towards them. God isn't different toward any of us.

The moment you start saying, "Well, why did God heal him? Why did God do this for him, yet He hasn't done it for me?" and you start thinking in those terms, you have to factor in your performance. You begin to acknowledge that you maybe haven't prayed enough or haven't done enough of this, or enough of that. You think your failures are why God hasn't done it. That's totally wrong thinking.

The grace of God is consistent. He's the same towards everybody. God is no respecter of persons. (Rom. 2:11.) He doesn't love one person more than He loves another. He hasn't provided more for one person than He's provided for another. By His grace, God has forgiven the sins of the entire human race. *Grace* is what God does for us, independent of us. Does that mean that everybody is saved? No, because not everybody has put faith in what God did by grace.

Prior to you existing, before you even had a need, God had already created the supply. Before you ever get discouraged, God has already blessed you with all spiritual blessings. He's already abounded towards you in love. You don't have to ask the Lord to give you joy and peace, to heal you, prosper you, and save you. He's already provided before you ever had the problem. That's awesome!

God, by grace, has already done everything. He anticipated every need that you could ever have, and He already met all of those needs through Christ. Through Jesus, God intervened in the affairs of men. He's provided everything, and that happened two thousand years ago. Jesus hasn't died for a single person's sins since. He hasn't healed a single person since He took our stripes on His back two thousand years ago.

Salvation, healing, and deliverance have already been provided. When people today hear this truth and believe, all of a sudden what God has already provided by grace becomes a reality to them. As they mix faith with the Word of God, what He has already done by grace begins to manifest in their life.

You're saved by grace through faith, not by one or the other exclusively. Understanding this foundational truth will make a huge difference in your life.

Poison

The balance of grace and faith is like sodium and chloride. Both sodium and chloride are poisons. If you take either one of them by themselves in sufficient quantity, they'll kill you. Yet if you mix sodium and chloride together, you get salt, a mineral necessary to sustain your life.

If all you do is emphasize faith, "You have to believe, and do this and that," that'll kill you spiritually. True Bible faith is simply your positive response to what God has already provided by grace. Faith only appropriates what God has already provided. Faith doesn't move God or make Him do anything.

If you don't recognize that faith is simply the way you appropriate and receive what God has already provided by grace, then the law and legalism will kill you. There are people who emphasize, "You have to pray, study, and believe God. You have to do something." They get so wrapped up in their performance that they think their "doing" is making God move. They see their faith as a pry bar—twisting God's arm and making Him perform. This begets legalistic thinking, and it'll destroy you. An inappropriate view of faith puts the entire burden on your shoulders. Faith or grace—independent of each other, not mixed together properly—will kill your walk with God.

This is the kind of background I came out of from previous churches I attended. We thought we had to do many different things in order to earn God's blessing. I didn't understand that the Lord had provided everything by grace. In fact, we used to have a little poem that said, "Mary had a little lamb, it would have been a sheep. But it joined our local church and died from lack of sleep." We just worked ourselves to the bone, doing all sorts of these things thinking our performance would move God's hand. Since then, I've realized that's not the way it works. There has to be a balance between grace and faith.

On the other end of the spectrum, many people in the Church emphasize grace alone saying, "It's just totally up to God." They say, "God is sovereign. Whatever He wills will be. Que sera, sera. It's just up to God." That kind of belief will kill you. I can personally name people who have died because of this belief system. They were just waiting on God to heal them, not understanding that they, too, had a part to play in receiving their healing.

Chapter 2

Is God Sovereign?

People have taken the truth that God moves independent of us, not based on our performance, and developed a teaching that is commonly called "the sovereignty of God." This teaching says that God just moves sovereignly, we have nothing to do with His actions whatsoever. This teaching overemphasizes grace.

They teach that God is sovereign and if it's His will, you'll be healed. If it's not, you'll die. It's just totally up to God. Some folks have taken this to the extreme. There are entire denominations that teach that certain people are predestined to salvation and others are predestined to damnation—and that God predetermined it. They believe that there's nothing you can do about it. It's just totally up to God.

The theological terms for this tension between grace and faith is *Calvinism* versus *Arminianism*. *Calvinism* emphasizes that everything is totally up to God. *Arminianism* emphasizes that you have a part to play, and that you can believe and receive, or doubt and do without. You can control the measure of the grace of God you experience by your faith. It's the Calvinists who emphasize this term, "the sovereignty of God."

Supreme, Independent, Excellent

The *New International Version* (NIV) popularized this term, *sovereignty*. In 288 verses of their translation, they substituted the phrase "Sovereign LORD" where it had previously been translated "Lord GOD" or "Lord God Almighty" in the *King James Version* (KJV) and others.

I'm not against applying this word—*sovereign*—to God if you'll use it the way the dictionary defines it. As a noun, it means "A king, queen, or other noble person who serves as a chief of state; a ruler or monarch" or "A gold coin formerly used in Great Britain" (*American Heritage Dictionary*). Of course, we're not talking about a coin.

As an adjective, the word *sovereign* speaks of something or someone being "Paramount or supreme." If you want to call God sovereign in the sense that He's paramount or supreme, I agree 100 percent.

Another definition is "having supreme rank or power." God is definitely at the top of the food chain. Nobody tells Him what to do. He is absolutely supreme.

Still another definition is "self-governing; independent." The United States is a sovereign nation. We broke away from the rule of Great Britain. You can apply this definition to God in the sense that God is sovereign. He's independent. Nobody gives Him orders.

Sovereign came from a Latin word that meant "super" or "above." I agree with that as it applies to God. In view of these dictionary definitions, I will agree that God is sovereign.

A Convenient Theology

But religion has come along and concocted its own definition of this word saying that *sovereign* means that God controls everything and that nothing can happen without His permission. I disagree with that interpretation. That's not what the Word of God teaches. God is not sovereign the way that certain religions have taught.

A person will die, and somebody will say, "Well, it must have been their time." They just think that nobody dies without it being "God's timing." I was leading the praise and worship at a Full Gospel Businessmen's meeting. The speaker had just come from the funeral of two teens who had been killed in an automobile accident. After drinking and doing drugs, they drove too fast on a slick, wet street, couldn't make a turn, and ran into a telephone pole. The accident killed both of them. A man in the gathering stood up and said, "Well, we know that God is sovereign. He works all things together for good, and He has a purpose in this. People can't die if it isn't God's will."

Most people have heard, said, or perhaps even embraced something similar to this at some point in their life. This is a convenient theology. When we don't understand certain things, it's easier to place full responsibility on God. Rather than put any responsibility on these teens, saying, "They shouldn't have been drinking, doing drugs, and speeding on a wet road. They killed themselves," we just say, "Well, it was God's will." No, it wasn't. People die all the time without it being God's will. It's not like God picks your number in heaven and you're just destined to die. The scriptures make very clear that Jesus came to...

…destroy him that had the power of death, that is, the devil.

Hebrews 2:14

Satan is the one who goes about seeking whom he may devour. (1 Pet. 5:8.) He's the one who comes to steal, kill, and destroy. (John 10:10.) God told us not to eat of the tree of the knowledge of good and evil because in the day that we ate thereof we would surely die. (Gen. 2:17.) We brought death into this life. We started old age, deterioration, sickness, and disease. God isn't the One who controls whether or not we become ill. We started the corruption on this planet. God doesn't control all of those things.

My father died when I was twelve years old. I remember our pastor coming over, sitting down, and looking at me, saying, "Andy, God needed your dad in heaven more than you needed him." Even as a twelve year old, I knew better than that! I thought, *What does God need my dad up in heaven for?* The Lord didn't kill my dad. This was just a cop-out, an easy way to deal with a difficult situation.

The Truth

In the very first church I pastored, there was a couple who gave birth to a child in a taxi on the way to the hospital. The baby was born not breathing, apparently dead. After going without air for a period of time, they finally revived the baby. This boy had Down syndrome and no immune system.

The boy only lived to be four years old. He died in my arms while I was praying for him. I then prayed for over two hours for him to be raised from the dead, but he didn't come back to life. I was struggling for some words that would minister to the family and to myself. As their pastor, I wanted so much to have something comforting to tell this couple. I was tempted to say, "Well, it must not be God's will," and just put the blame on God for the death of this child. God's big. He can handle it.

I was tempted, but I told that couple the truth, saying, "Look, God did not kill your child. This is not His will. I don't actually understand why we didn't see him healed and raised up from the dead. It's either due to my lack of faith, your lack of faith, or a combination of the two. Or, it might be because of things that I don't even understand. But I can guarantee you that God is not a baby killer."

Although it wasn't very comforting at the time, I just had to tell those people the truth. It would have been much more comforting to come across with something religious, saying, "God is sovereign. Nothing can happen but what God allows." But it's not the truth.

Ye shall know the truth, and the truth shall make you free.

John 8:32

Knowing the truth will make us free. The mother came back to me later and said, "I had a fear since the day he was born. They told me that he didn't have an immune system and if he ever got a cold, he would die." She told me, "I've dreaded this for four years. When I saw him get this cold, I just knew he was going to die." Because of her willingness to embrace the truth, the Lord showed her some things about herself and the situation. Because I didn't take the easy way out, but told her the truth, that woman discovered where the problem was, dealt with it, and had four more children.

The doctors told this woman never to conceive another child because she was too small to have children. If she did have more children, doctors said they would have to be delivered by C-section, and probably both she and the child would die. But because this woman was willing to embrace the truth, she believed God's Word and had four more children—all natural childbirths at home. No doctor would have let her deliver those children naturally after seeing her medical records, so she just believed God and had natural births at home. A few years ago, she sent me a picture of all four of her children in their caps and gowns as they graduated from college. She thanked me for telling her the truth.

Acts of God?

It's understandable to want to make everything fit in a nice little neat box, and to have an answer for everything saying, "Well, it must be God's will. He's sovereign." But this is not the truth, and believing lies will put you into bondage.

If God were guilty of everything He's blamed for today, there isn't a civilized nation on the face of the earth that wouldn't persecute, prosecute, and execute Him if He were a physical person. If God was the one making babies deformed, causing marriages to fail, and sending killer storms, the nations would kick Him out. If He really did cause all of the earthquakes, tornadoes, and other natural disasters we refer to in our contracts as "acts of God," every country would expel Him if they could. The truth is, God is being misrepresented, lied about, and blamed for things that aren't His doing.

This teaching that God sovereignly controls everything is the worst heresy in the body of Christ because it encourages passivism. If you really believe that God controls every single thing that happens, then what's the point of you doing anything? Why seek God? Why bother attending church meetings or conferences? Why not just stay at home sitting on your couch, eating candy and watching television, because God's will is going to come to pass anyway? Why do you need to do anything? God's will is going to come to pass whether you believe for it or not. That's a terrible doctrine!

Some people reject the extreme of this teaching, but they still mix it in to their belief system when it's convenient. When somebody dies, they say, "Well, it must be God's will." No, God isn't the One who causes death. Satan is the author of death, and we are the ones who loosed him in this earth. But to acknowledge our responsibility in this area is not always convenient.

The truth is, you can't just take part of this doctrine of sovereignty that is being taught and mix it together with faith. You can't say, "Well, I do have some responsibility, but there are some things that God just controls. He's sovereign in this area." No, either God controls everything, or He doesn't—that's the definition of *sovereignty*. He's either in control or He's not, there can be no combination of the two beliefs.

I've never understood people who get mad at me for preaching this truth. They say this teaching is of the devil. They ask me how I dare preach this. I ask them, if God controls everything and nothing can happen without Him either causing or allowing it, then I couldn't be preaching this if God didn't allow it, right? By their own doctrine, how can they be upset with me? It must be God's will for me to preach this. If God really controls everything, then He's leading me to say everything I'm saying, or I couldn't say it.

Defies Logic

If you truly believe that God controls everything, then when you get sick, why would you ever go to a doctor and try to get out of God's will? Why would you ever take medicine to lessen the pain? If God caused your sickness and He's trying to teach you something and work some redemptive purpose in your life, then why are you trying to lessen His work? Why not just learn your lesson and suffer to the max?

This defies logic. Nobody would believe this doctrine unless they're religious. You have to be taught this, and accept it on blind faith. It makes no sense. Even the people who say that God is putting sickness on them will go to the doctor and try to get out of "His will." Even those who are saying that God caused their marriage to fail will pray to God—who they say causes everything—and ask Him to intervene. Even those who say that God is the One who caused their financial problems and He's using the situation to humble them will pray and ask this same God for mercy and help. If you really believe that God sovereignly controls everything, then there is no point in doing anything because God's will is sovereignly coming to pass independent of us.

These beliefs bear no resemblance to the true definition of the word *sovereign*. They only represent a religious definition and application of this word.

Your Cooperation

God, by grace, has provided everything. But you have complete freedom of choice whether God's perfect will for you comes to pass or not. It doesn't happen without your cooperation.

> *Now unto him that is able to do exceeding abundantly above all that we ask or think...*
>
> Ephesians 3:20

Most people stop right there and believe this verse as is. However, they're skipping over the part that the entire verse hinges on.

> *...according to the power that worketh in us.*
>
> Ephesians 3:20

God cannot—or you could say does not—do anything beyond this power that works in you, which is faith.

Not Automatic

It is God's will for every single person to be saved.

> *The Lord is...not willing that any should perish, but that all should come to repentance.*
>
> 2 Peter 3:9

God, by grace, has already provided salvation for the whole world. But you have to put faith in God's grace to see this salvation come to pass. This verse makes it very clear that it is God's will for every person to be saved, but not every person is saved because not every person has responded in faith to what God has said. God's will does not come to pass automatically.

> *Enter ye in at the strait gate: for wide is the gate, and broad is the way, that leadeth to destruction, and many there be which go in thereat: Because strait is the gate, and narrow is the way, which leadeth unto life, and few there be that find it.*
>
> Matthew 7:13-14

Jesus said that there will be more people who enter in by the broad gate to destruction than by the narrow gate to everlasting life. The Lord Jesus Christ clearly said that not everybody will be saved, and yet 2 Peter 3:9 reveals that it is God's will for everybody to be saved. How can you put these scriptures together and come up with any other conclusion except that God's will does not automatically come to pass?

You have a choice. God, by grace, has provided everything. But if you don't believe, you won't receive.

Chapter 3

God's Will

God's will is for every person to be healed. Jesus is the perfect example of God's will.

> *God anointed Jesus of Nazareth with the Holy Ghost and with power: who went about doing good, and healing all that were oppressed of the devil; for God was with him.*
>
> Acts 10:38

What Jesus did was good, healing all who were oppressed of the devil. The Bible reveals that in the last days people will call evil "good" and good "evil" (Isa. 5:20). In Jesus' day, He said it was good that He healed the sick. Today, there are denominations who contend that healing the sick is of the devil. They're calling good "evil" and evil "good." Acts 10:38 reveals that it was the devil who was oppressing these people with sickness. Nowadays, entire denominations are saying, "When you get sick, it's God doing this to you. He's humbling you." They've totally flip-flopped, calling good "evil" and evil "good."

If you cannot discern between what God is doing and what the devil is doing, you won't know what to resist and what to yield to. If you don't understand these truths, how are you ever going to see the power of God manifested in your life or manifested in the life of others through you?

Deep Ruts

Are you blaming God for the tragedies in your life? James 1:2–4 says:

My brethren, count it all joy when ye fall into divers temptations; knowing this, that the trying of your faith worketh patience. But let patience have her perfect work, that ye may be perfect and entire, wanting nothing.

These verses have been twisted and misused to teach that God controls everything in your life. If someone hadn't already been prejudiced with that concept, they wouldn't get that out of these verses. It's like an old dirt road that wagons have been going up and down for years. The ruts are so deep you can't even begin to go down that road without slipping into them. Some of us have thought a certain way so long that when we hear something, we automatically transpose, translate, and interpret it in a way contrary to what the scripture is actually saying.

James 1:2–4 does not say that God puts troubles in your life to give you patience. Yet, that's what people teach out of these verses. "If you want patience, then be praying for trouble because tribulation works patience."

Enduring Faith

Romans 15:4 says:

For whatsoever things were written aforetime were written for our learning, that we through patience and comfort of the scriptures might have hope.

Notice it says "through patience and comfort of the scriptures." The scriptures are where patience comes from.

Patience is simply faith applied over a prolonged period of time. Instead of a momentary faith, patience is prolonged, enduring faith. Patience is when you just believe and keep believing. Romans 15:4 says that patience comes through the scriptures.

So then faith cometh by hearing, and hearing by the word of God.
Romans 10:17

Just as patience comes through the Word, so does faith. They are also both fruit of the Spirit.

But the fruit of the Spirit is…longsuffering [patience], …faith.
Galatians 5:22

When you were born again, God gave you faith and patience. They are fruit of your brand-new, born-again spirit.

Experiential Knowledge

Patience doesn't come through hardship. If it did, then the people who have suffered the most would be the most patient. That's not true. I defy you to show me that people who have had it the hardest are going to be the most holy, godly, and patient. Patience does not come through hardship and tribulation. However, if you already have patience through the Word of God and the fruit of the Holy Spirit on the inside of you, it has to be used before it reaches its full strength.

In 1969, I was drafted into the Army. They sent me through basic training to learn how to be a soldier—how to fire a weapon, throw hand grenades, and many other things. Once I arrived in Vietnam, I joked about people who were brand-new in the country because they were dangerous. All they had was head knowledge, they had never put into practice what they had learned. Even though these soldiers were trained the same as everyone else there, there's a depth of understanding about how to use that training that comes when you put it into practice. You become a better soldier when you are attacked and have to put your training into practice, than you were when you just went through basic training and only had intellectual knowledge. There's a difference between intellectual knowledge and experiential knowledge.

However, a soldier doesn't go looking for experiential knowledge. He doesn't stand up and say, "Right now, I know that all I have is intellectual knowledge. I really need someone to come along and attack me so that I can become a better soldier." Then when he sees the enemy coming, he doesn't run out to embrace and welcome them because this enemy has come to make him better. No, that's not how it works. You'll get killed doing that. The enemy does not come to make you better. They come to kill you.

Problems are not given by God to make you better. If you think they are, then you'll welcome and embrace those problems as being from the Lord. You'll attribute evil to God, which is wrong, and Satan will use that to kill you.

If you recognize that your problem isn't from God and say, "I'm going to fight this, and when I overcome it, I'll be stronger because I'll have put what I knew in my head into practice," then, yes, that's good. In fact, that's the whole point James 1:2–4 is teaching us. These verses aren't saying that God puts problems on you any more than it would make sense to say that an enemy comes against you to make you a better soldier. They come against you to kill you.

Passive

There are certain things you need to submit to, and others you need to resist.

> *Submit yourselves therefore to God. Resist the devil, and he will flee from you.*

> James 4:7

Extreme teaching on the sovereignty of God—where He controls everything—renders this verse useless. If God controls everything and nothing happens without Him willing or allowing it, then what's the purpose in resisting anything? It all came from God and if you resist it, you'll wind up resisting Him. This wrong understanding makes for passive Christians. Unfortunately, this currently describes the vast majority of the body of Christ.

When it comes to sickness, they waver. They say, "Maybe this is from God and maybe not. Lord, would You please heal me, if it be Your will?" They just throw their prayer out there, and if they get healed, then it must have been God's will. If they don't get healed, their number must have been up. What a stupid theology! Nobody's ever going to receive from God wavering like that.

Actively Fight Against

A certain preacher was asked if he tithed. He answered, "Sure I do. I take every offering I receive and put it in this big bucket. Then I throw it up in the air, praying, 'God, if You want anything, go ahead and take it. Whatever falls back to the ground is mine.'" You'll never give a tithe doing that. You have to be a little more deliberate.

To throw your prayer out there, saying, "God, if it's Your will, then heal me. If it's not, then it must be Your will that I'm suffering the way that I am," is just as senseless as trying to tithe by throwing your money up in the air and asking the Lord to take what He wants. It doesn't work that way. There are certain things that are from God. You submit to those. There are other things that are from the devil. You must resist those.

Resist means to actively fight against. If you don't actively fight against something, then you have submitted to it. Saying, "Dear Satan, please leave me alone," is not resisting the devil. You need to get angry and there's no way you can get angry if you think there is a possibility that God has a hand in your suffering.

The congregation of a little church I had begun pastoring wanted to invite a certain preacher to come and minister. I told them no because I didn't know him. They argued, "Well, he was here before you were." I agreed to listen to one of his previous messages on tape. In this message he taught on Romans 8:28, saying that everything comes from God.

This preacher admitted that he had a demonic lust in his heart for women. While preaching, he would be lusting after the women who were sitting in the auditorium. He said it got so bad that he finally told his wife. They decided to go for deliverance to have this demon cast out of him. As he went to get in his car to go to the appointment, he put his hand on the doorknob and a voice he attributed to God (I don't believe it was) spoke to him, saying, "You couldn't have this problem if I didn't allow it. I've sent this to teach you patience and to make you holier and better. If you get this demon cast out, you're going to thwart my will." So this preacher canceled his appointment and kept his demon because he felt that God had given it to him to make him better.

God Allowed It?

Most people would say that no way would God will for someone to keep a demon in their life. Well, it's all the same principle as believing that God would will for you to keep sickness, death, or lack in your life. How can you just interpret sovereignty this way up to a point, and then say, "Oh no, I don't believe that"?

I heard a woman being interviewed on television once. A man had abducted both she and her daughter at gunpoint. He took them out into a remote location and raped them. Then he laid both of them down on the ground and shot them in the back of the head, execution style. The daughter died, but the mother lived, despite having some physical problems because of the ordeal. There she was on television saying, "All things work together for good. God allowed it, and He's getting glory out of it."

Most of us would reject this thinking and say that God had no part in that. Why not? If God is truly sovereign in the religious sense of the word where He controls everything and nothing can happen without His permission, that means God is the One who's in charge of all the terrorist attacks, rapes, deformities, and problems in this world. You can't just accept this teaching when it's convenient to your situation and then say, "Beyond that, I believe it's impractical." No. Either it's true, or it isn't.

This teaching is not true. God doesn't control these horrible things, nor does He cause them. This passage from James 1 is saying that when you come into tribulation, rejoice. But not because God brought it. You must resist that tribulation knowing that it is from the devil, but it's an opportunity to put your faith to work. As you work your faith, you'll get experience, and experience will give you hope. You'll be stronger and better because you stood against, resisted, and fought the devil. But if you just sit there, roll over, and let these problems dominate your thinking, *Well, it must be God's will,* you aren't going to be better or stronger. You'll be destroyed by these tribulations.

Good God, Bad Devil

The religious teachings of today completely violate James 1:12–13.

Blessed is the man that endureth temptation: for when he is tried, he shall receive the crown of life, which the Lord hath promised to them that love him. Let no man say when he is tempted, I am tempted of God: for God cannot be tempted with evil, neither tempteth he any man.

Those religious teachings are saying that our temptation, hardship, trial, and persecutions are directly from God who is trying to build in us patience.

In context, these verses are really saying that these temptations, trials, and tribulations will help your patience become stronger as you put it into practice and exercise it like a muscle. But don't ever say that these temptations, trials, and tribulations are from God. Don't ever do that! Yet, the religious teachings today are preaching the exact opposite, saying that God is the source of tragedy. That's a faith-killer.

Jesus made it very clear:

The thief cometh not, but for to steal, and to kill, and to destroy: I am come that they might have life, and that they might have it more abundantly.

John 10:10

If it's good, it's God. If it's bad, it's the devil. God is a good God. The devil is a bad devil. Any time you get that confused, start embracing problems, and saying, "Oh God, I know You sent this to break me, humble me, and make me better," you have just crossed over into the extreme religious teaching on the sovereignty of God. It's a faith-killer. It will destroy you and render you useless.

Destroyed Relationship

People who think that the Lord's will is coming to pass with or without their input, have to blame God for the bad things that are happening in the world. They think it's God's fault that our nation is becoming increasingly ungodly and secular. They blame God for the abortion of more than 42 million babies in the U.S., thinking that they couldn't have been killed if it wasn't His will. Not only does this mind-set give you a skewed opinion of who God is, it'll destroy your relationship with Him as well.

If I were the one being blamed for sending hurricanes, tornadoes, tragedies, sickness, disease, divorce, heartbreak, and rebellious kids, would you want to be my friend? If you thought I was the one responsible for killing and maiming people, would you want to hang out with me? Yet religion says that God is responsible for all that stuff and then asks, "Don't you love Him?" We put on our most religious face and say, "Oh yes, I really love God," and then we duck, afraid that if we've done something wrong, He might put cancer on us to teach us a lesson because we deserve it. That's double-minded thinking and it's destroying people's relationship with God.

One of the leading media moguls in the United States owns a bunch of television networks. He was raised in a religious home. His sister died when they were children and the church people came over and told this boy, "God wanted your sister. It was His will that your sister died." This man said, "If there is a God, I hate Him for killing my sister." Today, he professes to be an agnostic and is doing all he can to change the Judeo-Christian ethics of the United States through his television networks. He's doing a fairly good job by introducing all kinds of ungodliness. Religious people represented the Lord as the One who killed his sister, and he turned against a God who would do that.

There are a lot of people in this nation who are turning against this God who is being represented as the One who sent the terrorist attacks, earthquakes, floods, and hurricanes. Religious leaders publicly attribute these things to the judgment of God. For example, Hurricane Katrina was attributed by some religious leaders to be the judgment of God. If the Lord started judging, He wouldn't have stopped at New Orleans. Hurricanes and other disasters are not the judgment of God. They are simply part of living in a fallen, sin-scarred world. As for Hurricane Katrina, the senseless plan of building a city below sea level and then building a large lake above the city held back by levies contributed to this catastrophe, too. It certainly wasn't God's fault.

Chapter 4

All Things Work Together for Good

We have been taught a false religious doctrine based on a misinterpretation of Romans 8:28. But if you would just read this verse in context and look carefully at the words, you wouldn't fall for such an erroneous interpretation. Many people who couldn't quote any other scripture in the Bible can quote Romans 8:28, which says...

And we know that all things work together for good to them that love God, to them who are the called according to his purpose.

People have interpreted this verse as saying that nothing can happen except what is in God's will. This verse does not say that! There is nothing in this verse that blames God for everything that happens. This verse simply says that the Lord can take whatever happens and work it together for good.

But there are qualifications. The very first word of this verse is the conjunction "and," which ties this verse to the previous verses. The preceding verses, verses 26 and 27, were saying that the Holy Spirit...

...helpeth our infirmities: for we know not what we should pray for as we ought...he maketh intercession for the saints according to the will of God.

The Greek word rendered "helpeth" literally means "to take hold of opposite together, that is, co-operate (assist):—help" (*Strong's Concordance*). It describes a union, not the Holy Spirit alone doing all the interceding for us. The Holy Spirit helps us as we are interceding, but He doesn't automatically do it for us. He takes hold together with us.

When we start doing what we know to do and we pray, if we will allow Him to do so, the Holy Spirit will take hold together with us and intercede and produce supernatural results. But this doesn't happen automatically. We have a part to play.

This is a significant departure from those who simply say that all things work together for good, regardless. No, all things do not work together for good if you aren't operating in intercession—not just a human intercession, but an intercession where you are energized by and operating in the power of the Holy Spirit. When the Holy Spirit gets involved and you are operating in supernatural intercession, then we can say that we know that all things will work together for good.

Them That Love God

There are two more qualifications in this verse. Verse 28 says that...

All things work together for good to them that love God...

Remember the two teenagers mentioned earlier in the book who died in the car accident? They were doing drugs and alcohol, missed a turn on wet pavement, and died. Those kids didn't love God. I'm not intentionally being mean toward them, I'm just stating the obvious based on their actions. (Luke 6:43–44.) The Bible calls a person who says that they love God but doesn't live like it, "a liar." (1 John 2:4; 4:20.) Doing drugs and alcohol, breaking the speed limit, going against the law of inertia (too fast around a corner)—say what you want, but there is no indication that these kids loved God.

The speaker at the Full Gospel Businessmen's meeting who had just been to the funeral of these kids said, "Well, we know that God took them." No, we don't know that. There are many people who die and go to hell. Not everyone who passes from this life automatically goes to be with the Lord. It depends on your decision whether or not you have accepted the salvation God has offered by His grace.

My wife, Jamie, and I were over in England when Princess Diana was killed in a car wreck. A denominational pastor was asked by one of the kids in his church, "Did Princess Diana go to heaven?" He answered, "Well, it depends on whether she knew God or not." The media twisted his words and plastered this headline on newspapers all over the UK, "Pastor Says Diana in Hell." People got mad! They were literally fearing riots and civil unrest in England because someone spoke the truth that if Princess Diana had not made Jesus her personal Lord, she went to hell.

No matter who someone is, if they haven't been born again before they die, they go to hell. It's not because of all their individual sins, but because they didn't make Jesus their personal Lord. That's the truth. But since the truth is potentially offensive, especially at a funeral, many people just take the easy route and say, "God is working this together for good, and we know they're in heaven," when it isn't necessarily true. There are consequences for your actions. You have to believe in order to receive.

Choose Life

This religious doctrine of the sovereignty of God is the same thing we see in the secular world where people are refusing to accept responsibility for their actions. Rather than admit that they have a problem with drinking, they say, "I can't help it. It's in my genes." It seems these days no one is responsible for anything. Just blame something, somebody, or everything—society, the color of your skin, where you grew up. If you can't find anybody else to blame, just blame your dysfunctional family.

But the Lord said in Deuteronomy 30:19…

I call heaven and earth to record this day against you, that I have set before you life and death, blessing and cursing: therefore choose life, that both thou and thy seed may live.

God not only gave you this quiz, He also gave you the answer—choose life. But notice, He gave you the choice. You must choose life. Satan didn't make you a jerk. You chose to be a jerk. You may have had some bad things happen in your life that made it harder on you than on somebody else, but nobody—even the devil himself—can do anything to you or make anything of you without your consent and cooperation.

According to modern psychology, I have little chance of being a normal adult male because my dad died when I was twelve years old. I grew up in a home without a father. Psychologists contend that I'm bound to have all kinds of problems. You might seriously wonder whether I'm normal or not, but my ninety-five-year-old mother told me recently that I never gave her a moment's problem. I didn't go through rebellion. I grew up loving my mother. I didn't realize that you had to be messed up if you didn't have a father. Nobody told me I had to have these problems.

Religious Counterpart

In our secular society today, nobody accepts responsibility for anything. It's always someone else's fault that you are the way you are. Instead of blaming the terrorists for their choice to kill thousands of people on September 11, 2001, some people are saying, "It's the United States that made these terrorists the way that they are." Give me a break!

The extreme teaching on the sovereignty of God is the religious world's counterpart to this secular world trend that refuses to accept responsibility for anything. We just blame God saying, "He's in control. All things work together for good." No, God didn't cause your problems, but yes, He can take those things and work them together for good. First, this is dependent upon the Holy Spirit interceding through you. Second, you have to love God.

The third qualification listed in Romans 8:28 for God turning all things to the good is…

...to them who are the called according to his purpose.

The purpose of God is to destroy the works of the devil.

For this purpose the Son of God was manifested, that he might destroy the works of the devil.

1 John 3:8

All things cannot work for the good if you aren't resisting the devil and fighting against the problems he sends. If you've embraced your situation, saying, "Oh God, thank You for giving me cancer," then don't think its going to work together for good. It only works together for good if you love God, are resisting the problem, and are out to destroy the works of the devil. If you will let the Holy Spirit work through you, then anything that the devil throws at you will work together for good.

Naptime

When my oldest son was just a year old, I was loading lumber one day to make a little bit of extra money. At the time, I was pastoring a church in Seagoville, Texas. It was hot, over a hundred degrees that day. The lumberyard was paved with dirt and Joshua had been out running and playing. When his naptime came, he wanted to lie down in this dirt and take a nap. He was sweaty from running around and I knew he'd be a mess if he lay down in the dirt. I also knew Jamie wouldn't like that, so I put him in the cab of the semi-truck we were loading. The window to the cab of the truck was up over my head.

When I put Joshua in there, I rolled the windows down and told him to lie down and take a nap.

Joshua, this once tired boy, revived when he got up in the cab of that truck. He'd been wanting to get up there all day long. He was now wide awake and looking out the window, waving at me in the rearview and side mirrors. I went up there and told him to lie down and take a nap. He disobeyed me and got up. Finally, I spanked him and told him to lie down and take a nap. Still Joshua leaned out of that window, trying to wave at me in the side view mirror again, then he fell out of that truck. He hit his eye on the running board and landed on his head on the ground. The fall could have broken his neck, killed him, or caused some other serious damage.

He was lying on the ground crying. I ran up and hugged him, held him, and prayed over him. When he finally quit crying, I said, "Joshua, this is what I was telling you. If you would have obeyed me, this wouldn't have happened." I used that negative circumstance to teach him a lesson.

If my son would have been like most Christians, he would have gone out and told all of his friends, "My dad is such a wonderful dad! He pushed me out of the cab of that truck, gave me a black eye, and made me land on my head to teach me to obey him." If anybody could prove that a parent does stuff like that, the welfare department would come, take you away, and lock you up because that is not the right way to discipline your children. Yet this is what many Christians are saying God does.

A Real Faith-Killer

There is a famous quadriplegic minister who blames God for their condition, but the truth is that this person jumped off a rock into a pool of water that had a sign there stating, "Do Not Swim." They went ahead, disobeyed, broke their neck, and became quadriplegic. They then say, "God did this to me to get my attention."

There is no doubt that God used this situation because this person turned to Him while lying there, a quadriplegic with nothing else to do but listen to God. This person now praises the Lord for doing this and leads many people to Him, but God didn't cause or allow that accident. That's a misrepresentation. The Lord didn't do it.

If all you do is emphasize grace and say, "It's just totally God's will. We can't affect His plans. God's will automatically comes to pass. We have nothing to do with it," then instead of embracing true biblical grace, you're now embracing an extreme religious teaching on the sovereignty of God. Thinking that God controls everything and nothing happens without His permission is a real faith-killer.

If you really believe that, just go out and live in sin because after all, you couldn't do it if it wasn't God's will. Go out and be as carnal as you want to because you couldn't do it if the Lord didn't will it. When put in those terms, this thinking defies logic. Only a religious person with a blinded heart would believe that. It's not true. That kind of thinking emphasizes a few scriptures that talk about God being all-powerful and knowing the end from the beginning, and then takes them to an unbalanced extreme.

Chapter 5

God Is Not Your Problem

Although it's a major doctrine in the body of Christ, there are only two places in scripture where predestination is mentioned: Romans 8:29–30 and Ephesians 1:5 and 11. Some people, however, believe that God has predestined everything.

Romans 8:29 says:

> *For whom he did foreknow, he also did predestinate to be conformed to the image of his Son, that he might be the firstborn among many brethren.*

The key to understanding predestination is to understand that God only predestined those whom He foreknew. Foreknowledge refers to God's ability to know the future. Only people He already knew would accept Jesus have been predestined. Nobody has been predestined to be saved or lost. But once you become born again, God has predetermined—predestined—that you will be conformed to the image of His Son. If you don't cooperate in this life, then it will happen when He comes.

When we see Jesus…

We shall be like him; for we shall see him as he is.

1 John 3:2

If you will cooperate with the Lord, then you can start being like Him here in this life. You can start walking in joy, peace, victory, anointing, and power. If you've been born again, it's predetermined that you will ultimately be like Jesus. If you'll cooperate, you can experience that here in this life to the degree that you renew your mind. If you don't cooperate, you'll eventually be like Jesus anyway because you'll be like Him when He comes. You're predestined to be. That's all that verse means.

Good Plans

God didn't predestinate anyone to be a mess. He didn't predetermine anybody to be a failure.

For I know the thoughts that I think toward you, saith the LORD, thoughts of peace, and not of evil, to give you an expected end.

Jeremiah 29:11

God has good plans for you. He has a plan and a destiny for every person. You didn't happen accidentally. Whether your parents knew you were coming or not, God knew. He has a plan for you, and He didn't plan for anyone to be mediocre or a failure. God didn't plan the hurt and heartache that you've experienced. He didn't plan the tragedy. If you had a terrible childhood, it wasn't God who caused that to happen. It happened because people made poor choices using the free will God gave them.

People have made wrong choices and sometimes you suffer because of those choices, but God didn't determine this. He doesn't control people like chess pieces and make everything happen. If you've had terrible tragedies happen in your life, God didn't cause them.

I take great comfort in knowing that God is a good God. My dad died when I was twelve years old, but God didn't kill him. I've had a lot of negative circumstances happen in my life. I've been stolen from, lied about, kidnapped, blacklisted, spit on, and much, much more. Those things happened to me, but God didn't order them. He's not the One who caused my problems. At the very least it was the devil, and at least half the time, I was cooperating somehow to bring them to pass. It blesses me to know that God is not my problem.

God is not your problem either. It's just not all up to Him. Grace is what God does for you independent of you, but you don't experience the goodness of God's grace in your life unless you learn some things and know how to cooperate with Him. As you continue reading this book, you'll learn more truths which will help you better understand what is God's part and what is your part. Grasping these truths will help you put your faith in what God has done instead of mistakenly placing your faith in what you have done. It will help you understand the power and authority that God has given you, and will give you some answers that will really make a difference in your life.

Reach Out and Take It

In my own personal life, if I hadn't corrected my understanding, I never would have seen anywhere near as much as I have. The things of God don't come to pass automatically. If you don't pursue them, you won't get them. You must pursue the things of God.

Take, for instance, the baptism in the Holy Spirit. Many people have told me, "If God wants me to receive the baptism in the Holy Spirit and speak in tongues, I'm ready. It's just up to Him. If He wants to give it to me, I'll get it." That's not how it happens. You can't just say, "If God wants me to be saved, I'll receive. It's just up to Him." No, you must believe!

I remember sitting in the very back of the church auditorium one day as a boy in Vacation Bible School. The man up front took something out of his wallet and announced, "I'll give this dollar bill to the first kid who comes up here and takes it." Instantly, there were twenty or thirty kids jumping up and down around him saying, "I want it, I want it!" I was thinking, *This is the worst time to be sitting in the back row* (my family normally sat in the front). However, this guy ignored those kids, kept his hand up in the air, and repeated, "I'll give this dollar bill to the first kid who comes up here and takes it." All of us in the crowd were wondering, *What's he saying?* All of those kids up there jumping around him wanted it.

After he had said a third time, "I'll give this dollar bill to the first kid who comes up here and takes it," it finally hit me what he meant. I leaped off of my chair and ran all the way down to the front. Pushing my way through those kids, I grabbed the man's arm, climbed up his side, and snatched the dollar bill out of his hand. When I did, he looked at me and said, "Now you're the first kid who came up here and took it." Looking at the other kids, he said, "All of you wanted it, and it was available, but you have to reach out and take it." Then he taught us how receiving salvation is like that.

God has already provided the forgiveness of sins for every person, but it doesn't just automatically come to pass. It's not just grace alone that saves you. You must believe. You have to reach out and take hold of your salvation. You must come against the thoughts that the devil puts in your mind saying, "God couldn't love you that way. You're too ungodly," and so on. You have to fight through those things and persevere. You must reach out and by faith declare, "I believe what God's Word says," and take hold of the grace God is offering. It doesn't come to pass automatically.

It's Your Choice

The principle is the same with everything else in the Christian life. God has already made provision. How long will you sit there, saying, "Que sera, sera. Whatever will be, will be," all the while blaming God for the mess your life is in? It is time for you to stand up and declare, "The Lord has provided something better for me than this. Praise God, I'm going to find out what my part is, do what God has told me to do, and receive His miraculous power." It's your choice.

Chapter 6
The Response of Faith

Both grace and faith need to be combined to be able to see the power of God released in your life. The body of Christ as a whole is divided between those who emphasize grace alone at the exclusion of faith and those who emphasize faith alone at the exclusion of grace. Emphasizing either one—grace or faith—is wrong if you take them independent of the other.

> *For by grace are ye saved through faith; and that not of your-selves: it is the gift of God.*
>
> Ephesians 2:8

It's the combination of grace and faith together that releases the power of God. Grace or faith taken by themselves at the exclusion of the other is actually disastrous and will destroy you.

Many people have emphasized that everything is just up to God to the exclusion of the truth that we have a part to play in what He does. This extreme teaching of the sovereignty of God—where people blame Him for every single thing that happens to us—is the worst doctrine in the body of Christ today. It just renders people passive. If God is controlling everything, what's the point of seeking Him, praying, studying the Word, or doing anything, because after all, it's just up to God. A large segment of the body of Christ is stuck in this thinking and it is keeping us from taking our authority.

Resist the Devil

James 4:7 says:

Submit yourselves therefore to God. Resist the devil, and he will flee from you.

You must recognize that some things are from God and some things are from the devil. Satan is not God's messenger boy. This mental image that the devil is on a leash and God only lets him go so far, isn't true. You are the one who allows Satan to come in.

*Your adversary the devil, as a roaring lion, walketh about, seeking whom he **may** devour.*

1 Peter 5:8

Satan cannot devour everybody. He can't do things to you without your consent and cooperation. One of the things that turns the devil loose in your life is the attitude that things can't happen unless it is God's will. This thinking leads you to believe that you can't really fight against it. James 4:7 tells us to "resist the devil." *Resist* means to actively fight against. You cannot actively fight against something if you think God has ordained or permitted it. He's not the One who permits these things.

Unbelief Limits God

Consider when the Israelites came out of the land of Egypt. There are many, many instances where the Lord made it clear that He wanted them to enter directly into the Promised Land and receive the promises He had for them. But because of their disobedience and unbelief, they spent forty years in the wilderness. That wasn't God's will or plan for them.

> *Yea, they turned back and tempted God, and limited the Holy One of Israel.*
>
> Psalm 78:41

In their hearts, they turned back to Egypt, tempted God, and limited the Holy One of Israel. Many people can't even conceive of this. They think, *There's nothing we can do to limit God.* But keep in mind, the Lord is not forcing His will upon us individually or collectively as a nation or group of people. You have to cooperate with God to see His will come to pass in your life.

Deuteronomy 7:15–18 talks about how the Israelites would have absolute victory. Nobody would stand before them. The Lord would deliver all of their enemies into their hands—this is a promise of complete victory. Verse 17 says:

> *If thou shalt say in thine heart, These nations are more than I; how can I [God] dispossess them?*

God had just promised them absolute victory. He told them that nobody would be able to stand before Israel. They would win every battle. Everything is going to work. But God then tells the Israelites that if they refuse to believe that victory is theirs, if they get into unbelief, He would be unable to dispossess the enemy nations.

God cannot bring deliverance in your life if you yield to fear and doubt through unbelief. That stops the power of God from operating. This is a very important truth, but to those who emphasize the extreme sovereignty of God—that He controls everything—what I've just shared is terrible. These people hate me for teaching this. I've been branded a cult and all kinds of things because I preach that God's will doesn't just automatically come to pass. You have to choose God's will. Personally, I think this is obvious if you are a student of the Word.

Not in Vain

Paul said:

> For I am the least of the apostles, that am not meet to be called an apostle, because I persecuted the church of God.
>
> 1 Corinthians 15:9

That's a strong statement coming from a man who wrote half of the New Testament and saw people raised from the dead. Paul was a powerful man of God, yet he knew that wasn't because of who he was in the natural. It was because of the grace and mercy of God. So he said, "I'm the least, not even fit to be called an apostle, because of the things I did."

But verse 10 goes on to say:

> But by the grace of God I am what I am...

He gave all of the credit to God and said, "It's the grace, the unmerited favor and ability of God, that was given to me that made me who I am." Then he continued saying:

> ...*and his grace which was bestowed upon me was not in vain.*
>
> 1 Corinthians 15:10

In Galatians 2:16, Paul said that if you are trying to be justified by the works of the law, then Christ profits you nothing. Your faith is vain and you make void the grace of God.

Grace is what God does for us, independent of us. It has nothing to do with our performance. By grace, God has already provided forgiveness of sins, healing, deliverance, joy, and peace. Everything has already been accomplished by the grace of God. But grace alone does not transform us unless there is the response of faith on our part. This is what the apostle Paul was saying.

I Labored More Abundantly

> *His grace which was bestowed upon me was not in vain; but I laboured more abundantly than they all: yet not I, but the grace of God which was with me.*
>
> 1 Corinthians 15:10

This verse serves as a great example of grace and faith working together. God, by grace, extended a call to Paul. He was on his way to murder Christians in Damascus, yet Jesus appeared to him in a blinding flash of light and gave him an opportunity to respond. That was grace. Paul didn't deserve that. When the Lord spoke to him, He said:

> I am Jesus whom thou persecutest: it is hard for thee to kick against the pricks.
>
> Acts 9:5

The Lord had already been convicting Paul and pricking his heart. There are several scriptures that recount where people were pricked in their hearts (Acts 2:37, for example). This is speaking of the conviction of the Holy Spirit.

God had been convicting Paul ever since he saw Stephen stoned to death. Saul, who became Paul, was the one at whose feet everybody laid their coats down. He kept their garments as he watched them stone Stephen to death. (Acts 7:58.) Saul saw Stephen as he was dying, kneel down and pray:

> Lord, lay not this sin to their charge.
>
> Acts 7:60

Stephen saw the heavens open up and saw Jesus standing at the right hand of God. (Acts 7:55–56.) Saul heard Stephen testify of this moments before he was killed, and God had been pricking Saul's heart ever since. The Lord extended grace toward the man who was killing His own people. That's the grace of God!

A Spiritual Battle

If Paul hadn't responded and labored more abundantly than they all, then we might have read the report about how Saul became converted, but he wouldn't have ever become Paul. He wouldn't have been the apostle who wrote half of the New Testament and did all of these great miracles. It takes a response on our part for God's grace and what He's freely provided for us to be able to work in our life.

We are in a battle! I'm amazed how many people don't understand this. They're looking for physical, natural reasons why everything happens, but we are in a spiritual battle and Satan is doing everything he can to stop you. You look at things in the natural realm, wondering, *Why this?* That's the reason people fall into despair when they see the political process go differently than what they want. It's because that is where their hope and faith are rather than in God. They are looking to physical, natural things as their salvation. But there is a spiritual battle going on.

When you cooperate with God and seek Him with your whole heart, good things happen. When you don't seek God and you're operating in the carnal realm, bad things happen because Satan is always going about seeking whom he may devour. It takes your consent and cooperation for the devil to do anything in your life. Not many people believe that, but it's true.

We aren't fighting flesh and blood. Ours is not a physical battle; it's a spiritual battle involving spiritual dynamics, and you have to cooperate. You must resist—fighting the unbelief, discouragement, and negativism of this world—to see what God wants to accomplish in your life come to pass.

God has a perfect plan for every one of us. He hasn't made a single one of us for defeat or failure. He has a perfect plan for everyone, but only some people will see these plans come to pass in their life. It's not because God created some of us to be duds. It's not because He wants some of us to be failures. It's not because there are only a few people that God really loves. No, the grace of God is the same toward every person, but not everybody labors abundantly to bring to reality God's purpose and plan for their life.

Go for It!

Some people have had the Lord speak a word to them, yet here they are a year, two years, even three years later still not doing what God told them to do. I just can't understand that. I don't even want to understand that. If God tells me to do something, I'll do it!

We offered one of our Bible college graduates a job running our night school. At the time, the night school position was just a part-time job, and this young man was used to making a lot of money. He has a large family—five kids—and it was going to be a big cut in pay for him if he accepted the position. While he was out at my house doing some things, he said, "I really feel that this is what God wants me to do, but I have a family to take care of. This is like half of the salary that I had. What do I do?" He was asking me all kinds of questions. I just told him, "You lost me when you said that this is what you feel God wants you to do. If you truly believe that this is what God wants you to do, then just do it."

"Well, what about…?"

I answered, "I don't care about anything else. If you have to get rid of some things, downsize, sell your house, move into an apartment, sell your cars—whatever you have to do just do what God tells you to do."

This man decided to take the job, but it was about four or five months until the position actually opened up. During that time, there were many changes in the personnel at our Bible college and we ended up promoting this young man to a different position which paid nearly identical wages to the job he was leaving. He didn't lose a thing! But if he had not agreed to that part-time position, we probably wouldn't have hired him for the higher paying, full-time position.

Some people hear God's voice, but then they debate, saying, "But God, what about this?" Who cares about anything else? This is not a dress rehearsal. This is the real deal. If God speaks to you and tells you something, you ought to drop everything else and do whatever it is that He says. If the Lord said it, that ought to be it. God has a plan for your life that is superior to anything you could ever plan on your own. You need to follow Him.

What a privilege it is to hear the voice of God. What an honor it is to have God Almighty speak to you. When He does, just lay aside everything else and follow.

Misplaced Priorities

A woman once told the director of our school, "I know that God has called me to come to Colorado Springs and go to Charis Bible College, but I have two dogs. What do I do?"

He answered, "The last time I checked they allow dogs in Colorado. Bring them with you."

I told her, "Get rid of them." Now I'm a dog lover, and I've had dogs myself. But if a dog was getting in the way of me doing what God had told me to do, I would turn that dog loose or give it to another family. I'd do anything it took. Why in the world would you let two dogs—or whatever it is for you—keep you from obeying God? That's misplaced priorities.

God has a will for you. He extends grace, but there must be some effort on your part. You have to make some decisions. You need to do whatever it takes to follow God, balancing grace and faith. God, by grace, gives us giftings, talents, and abilities that are completely independent of anything we deserve. It's just grace. These things are God's part. He moves by grace. But then there is a required response of faith on our part necessary to bring God's will to pass in our lives. You must merge these two together in the proper mixture to be able to see the power of God operate in your life. Don't get ahead of God and start making decisions on your own, trying to force Him to do things; that's not going to work either. You need to discover what God has done by grace—what He's provided, what His will is. Then there needs to be an appropriate response on your part, which is what the Bible calls faith.

Chapter 7
Making God Move

Faith is simply our positive response to what God has already done by grace. Faith is not something you do to get God to respond. This is a major misconception in the body of Christ among those who emphasize faith.

They often take scriptures like Mark 11:23, and only emphasize what you have to do. Some have even come up with the opinion that they are forcing God, that they're making God move. This is how we came up with such statements as, "Faith moves God." God isn't the one who's stuck. He's not the one who needs to move. God moved before you ever had a problem. He moved through Jesus. Every person who will ever be healed was healed two thousand years ago through Jesus. Every person who will ever be saved was already forgiven two thousand years ago through Christ. Every person who will ever be blessed, have joy, peace or whatever, it's already been done two thousand years ago through Jesus.

You don't need God to move. You don't need Him to come and touch you or heal you. God has already provided everything. You can't make

Him do anything. If your attitude is, "I'm going to make God heal me, I'm going to make the power of God flow," that's arrogance gone to seed. It will cause frustration in your life as you try to twist God's arm and force Him to do something. That's not consistent with the Word at all.

Faith Appropriates

Faith doesn't move God. He has already moved by grace. Faith is just your positive response to what you believe God has already provided. Faith only appropriates what God has already provided by grace. If God hasn't already provided it by grace, then your faith can't make it happen.

> *For verily I say unto you, That whosoever shall say unto this mountain, Be thou removed, and be thou cast into the sea; and shall not doubt in his heart, but shall believe that those things which he saith shall come to pass; he shall have whatsoever he saith. Therefore I say unto you, What things soever ye desire, when ye pray, believe that ye receive them, and ye shall have them.*
>
> Mark 11:23–24

This passage has been taught repeatedly by people who emphasize faith. They say, "We have power and authority, and there are certain things that we have to do to see God's will come to pass." That's true, but it can be taken to an extreme—to the point that you believe you can literally "make" God do anything. "Whatsoever you want, just say it! Believe that you receive, and God has to do it." You'll hear people use that kind of terminology as they say, "We're going to grab hold of God and not let go until we make the power of God flow."

We see this in the body of Christ right now with much of the prayer and intercession for revival. People believe that God is up there with His arms folded, thinking, *You bunch of hypocrites!* They say, "God isn't moving or pouring out His power on people to be saved, healed, and delivered because He's upset with us. So what we must do is get people together to pray and repent. But He won't listen to just one or two of us. We have to have hundreds of thousands, even millions of people praying. We have to put pressure on God and stay after Him. Let's get on a twenty-four hour chain and not let go until we just literally badger God and make Him release His power and pour out revival!" They might not use those exact words, but that is the attitude that is prevalent in the body of Christ—that we are making God move and pour out His power. That's an affront to God! It's implying that you love people more than He does!

Be a Channel

Earlier in my life, I participated in all of these things that I'm teaching against now. I myself have done them, so I have an understanding and compassion for people who are doing what I'm speaking against. But since then, I've grown and matured in God's Word and I no longer do those things I once did. I remember leading "all night" prayer meetings that never lasted past one or two in the morning. That's before we could pray in tongues. You can pray for the whole world in thirty minutes if you don't know how to pray in tongues!

I remember praying so hard that I was literally screaming, yelling, and pounding my fist against the wall. I said, "God, if You love the people in Arlington, Texas, half as much as I do, we would have revival!" As soon as that left my lips, I knew that something was seriously wrong with my theology. I was trying to get God to be as compassionate as I was, which is exactly what many people do in prayer. They say, "Oh God, don't You care about our country? Oh Lord, why are You pouring Your Spirit out over in Africa? Why don't we see very many miracles? Oh God, please move here!" It's like we honestly don't believe that God loves people as much as we do. Something is seriously wrong with that kind of thinking.

When you intercede for someone, perhaps your spouse or children, do you pray in such a way that you imply that you love them more than the Lord does? Why would you approach Him that way? It's because you don't believe that God has already done His part. You think He's waiting until somebody rises up and prays, and then He responds to your prayer with action. That's wrong, but it's the way most people are thinking today. That's you taking too much responsibility, and thinking that you can make God move.

At a recent meeting, a woman came up to me saying, "I know the Lord hears your prayers. Would you please pray that God would move and save my husband?"

I answered, "What do you want me to pray? How can I get God any more motivated to save your husband than what He already is? He already sent His Son to die for you. You're implying that God isn't as motivated as I am." I told this woman, "You're approaching this whole thing wrong. Instead of approaching God as an adversary and trying to make Him do something, you ought to start praising God that He loves your husband more than you do. You ought to start praising

God for the great things He's done, and just be a channel of His love flowing towards your mate."

Whatsoever You Desire

Many people err, trying to force God to do something. They take scriptures like Mark 11:24, and say, "I confess with my mouth and believe with my heart that I can rob a bank and get away with a million dollars without being caught." After all, doesn't Mark 11:24 say "whatsoever"? Isn't robbing a bank a "whatsoever"? Of course, most people don't believe you can use scripture to get away with robbing a bank, but you need to understand why that isn't true. Why can't we use Mark 11:24 to go rob a bank?

A certain woman started a faith-oriented Bible school in Arlington, Texas. What she desired was to be the wife of well-known evangelist and Bible teacher Kenneth Copeland. So she put on a wedding gown and had an actual wedding ceremony where she "married" Kenneth Copeland "in the spirit." Of course, he wasn't physically there. But she stood on Mark 11:24 and "married him in the spirit." She desired Kenneth Copeland to be her husband, so she confessed it and "stood" on this scripture in "faith" for it.

The problem was, Kenneth was already married to Gloria Copeland. This lady in Arlington viewed Gloria as her mountain, so she cursed her and commanded her to die so she would get out of the way. She went ahead and "married" Kenneth "in the spirit," and she was just waiting for Gloria to die so she could go ahead and consummate the marriage with Kenneth. That was over thirty years ago. This "consummation" hasn't happened yet, and it isn't going to happen.

Most people would say that this woman was way off in her belief. That this scripture does not apply to her situation. Why not? The Bible clearly says "whatsoever things you desire." Isn't wanting somebody else for a mate a "whatsoever"? Isn't that a desire? The Word says that whatsoever things you desire when you pray, believe that you receive them and you shall have them. This is a promise. Why can't you claim another person? Why can't you curse their mate and command them to die? The answer to this is found in the balance of grace and faith.

Faith only appropriates what God has already provided by grace. If God hasn't already provided it, your faith can't make God do anything. The reason you can't go out and successfully rob a bank using Mark 11:24 is because God didn't provide for thievery in His atonement. Grace hasn't already provided the means to steal from others. The reason you can't curse another person and command them to die and then marry their mate is because God didn't provide for murder and adultery in His atonement. Mark 11:24 doesn't make God do anything. It's talking about discovering what He's already provided. Then, if you will believe, your faith will reach out and appropriate what God has already provided by His grace. If you could just understand that, it would revolutionize your relationship with God.

A Totally Different Attitude

Many people are trying to get God to do something. They're struggling to receive, saying, "I'm trying to believe God that He'll do this."

Once you understand the balance of grace and faith, it takes the struggle out of receiving from God. How can you doubt that God will do what He's already done? If it's done by God's grace, then it's already done. Grace is not something that is going to happen. It's something that has already been done. Jesus already died for the sins of the whole world. He's already died to provide forgiveness of our sins, the healing of our bodies, and the deliverance from all these things. It's already done. If Jesus has already died for you and it's already done—"by whose stripes ye were [past tense] healed" (1 Peter 2:24)—how can you doubt that He will do what He's already done? This understanding takes all the struggle out of it.

Many people go to a meeting saying, "Oh God, I'm just believing that You're going to heal me. I know You're going to heal somebody, and I'm believing that You'll heal me. I'm believing for You to heal me." There's an element of doubt in those words. There is uncertainty and anxiety. If it hasn't already happened, then there's a possibility that it won't.

When you come to a meeting say, "Father, I thank You that I've already been healed. It's already been done. I know it's mine, and hallelujah, I'm receiving." There's a totally different attitude in a person who is just trusting and relying upon what God has already done versus someone who is trying to get God to do something.

Really, the audacity of people to think that we can make God do things defies logic. Yet this is basically where religion is today. Religion is trying to force God in a myriad of ways. So we don't believe He'll do it for one, two, or ten people, then get a hundred million. "If we could get so many people praying at the exact same moment, that would put pressure on God and make Him move." Nonsense! That's not what these scriptures are teaching.

Quit Trying, Start Trusting

We need to understand that God, by grace, has already done everything. And if He's done it, then it's just a matter of resting in what He's already done. It's just a matter of reaching out by faith to receive it. When you realize that by the stripes of Jesus you're already healed, then it's easy to say, "If I'm already healed, then that means in the spirit realm I already have this power on the inside of me. Instead of struggling, Lord, I'm just going to rest in what You've already done. It's a done deal."

You need to quit trying to get healed and start trusting that you've already been healed. There's a huge difference between the two.

When Jamie and I first started out in the ministry, we were so poor that we couldn't even pay attention. We really struggled financially, and it was my own fault. At times, Jamie and I would go weeks without eating much.

The Bible I was using to pastor my first church was one that I had taken with me through my days as a soldier in Vietnam. It was a mildewed mess! I had written all over in it and had taped nearly every page to keep it together. Entire books—not just chapters, but books—of the Bible were gone. They'd fallen out. Many times I would open my Bible and say, "Let's turn over to…" and the book I was looking for wasn't there. I'd just have to quote the passage from memory. That's one reason I can quote so many scriptures. I had to remember passages because I didn't even have a whole Bible.

Finally, I decided that I just had to believe God and start seeing some of these truths work somewhere in my life. I drew a line in the sand and declared, "This is it! I believe God for a new Bible." You might have a hard time relating to this but honestly, it took me six months to believe for an extra twenty dollars so that I could buy a Bible. You may think, *Well, that's just a matter of priorities. You were using your money for other things.* When Jamie and I were first married, our entire income for the first twelve months of our marriage was $1,253. We paid $100 a month rent plus utilities. I don't know how that works! Our second year's income jumped up to $2,500 over twelve months. So we made a total of $3,753 in twenty-four months. We were struggling, to say the least. When I say it took me six months to believe for twenty extra dollars for a Bible, know that I was putting a very high priority on it.

You've Already Got It

During that period of time, I struggled. Satan was telling me, "You'll never get a new Bible. It will never work!" For me, I felt that our ministry was going to stand or fall based on whether or not I could believe God for this twenty extra dollars to go purchase a Bible. After six months, I finally had enough money so I went and bought a Bible. I had my name engraved on it. When I walked out of that bookstore with that Bible under my arm, instantly I quit doubting that I'd get it.

Prior to that time, there wasn't ten minutes during my waking hours that I didn't have some fear, anxiety, or thought of unbelief that my faith would not work. I continually thought, "You can't get it.

Some man of God you are. You can't even believe for a Bible!" I had to deal with such thoughts constantly. But as soon as I had that Bible in my hand, I quit doubting that I'd get it. You're probably thinking, *Well of course! Why would you doubt that you're going to get it if you've already got it?* That's my point exactly.

Are you sitting there saying with your mouth, "I'm healed," but then your next thought is, *I'm going to die. I don't know if I'll ever get better. What will my funeral be like?* Then you catch yourself and say, "No, in the name of Jesus." The reason you waver so in your faith and deal with all these thoughts is because you are thinking that God will respond to your faith and heal you. If only you could understand that God healed you before you ever became sick, before you were ever born, before you ever had a problem—God has already healed you. According to Ephesians 1:19–23, the same power that raised Jesus Christ from the dead already dwells in you. You have raising-from-the-dead power at your disposal. Jesus gave you the authority to use this power to speak to this mountain and command it to be removed. Once you understand that God has already done it, how can you doubt that He'll do what He's already done?

If you're struggling and saying, "Well, I'm trying to believe, but I just don't know if I'll ever get healed," it's because you don't understand that faith just appropriates what God has already provided. You are still thinking that God is going to respond to you—that when you do every-thing correctly, including holding your mouth just right and confessing so many times, then God will release His power. You still think that God is responding to your faith. No, your faith is a response to God's grace. When you get those things mixed up, you'll always be frustrated.

Chapter 8
Already Provided

I came out of the "faith movement," so I'm not against it. There were many great truths revealed to me through that teaching, and I'm still a "faith person" today. But many people didn't understand that faith just appropriates what God has already provided. They made faith into a work—something they did trying to force God to move—and so they became frustrated. There are thousands of faith people who aren't part of a local church today because they became frustrated. They did everything they knew and were taught to do. They pushed every button, but God didn't come through. They feel like the Lord failed them because they did these things but God didn't respond the way they were told He would. This whole problem is eliminated when you understand that faith only appropriates what God has already provided.

You aren't trying to get God to do anything. It's not about God giving, it's all about you learning how to receive. Once you understand that, it makes the Christian life so simple. The reason you study the Word isn't so you can earn a star that you can then turn in, in exchange for an answer to prayer. It's not going to earn you any favor with God. You study the Word so you can learn what God has already done, what God has already provided. As you learn about your great salvation, faith just rises up on the inside and you start believing God. This is infinitely better in that it will give you peace in your relationship with God.

Even then, there will probably still be some things that you believe God has provided by grace that you aren't seeing come to pass in your life. When that happens, just keep renewing your mind to the Word. God's Word works, but renewing your mind is a process.

People come up to me and say, "I'm just angry at God because He failed to do this." I don't even relate to that. God has never failed to do anything. If anyone failed, it was me who failed to understand, appropriate, and receive. I had wrong attitudes that hindered what God wanted to do. The Lord has never failed me. If anything, I've failed God, but He has never failed me.

Back in those poverty days I spoke of previously, it wasn't God who was failing to meet our needs. I failed to understand the Word concerning how to receive to have my needs met. I was under the impression that I would be sinning against God if I worked a secular job. I was called to the ministry and thought I had to get all my money from ministry, but eventually I learned better. I was hindering God's supply—which I wanted so desperately—by my failure to work.

Once you understand that God by grace has already done everything, you can get rid of this wrong attitude. He's provided everything that you will ever need. If you understand these truths, they'll transform your life. God has already done His part. We aren't trying to get Him to do anything. You don't have to badger God and plead with Him.

Not a Comparison

Many people have misunderstood what Jesus was communicating in Luke 11. After teaching on what's commonly called "The Lord's Prayer," He told a parable, saying:

> *Which of you shall have a friend, and shall go unto him at midnight, and say unto him, Friend, lend me three loaves; for a friend of mine in his journey is come to me, and I have nothing to set before him? And he from within shall answer and say, Trouble me not: the door is now shut, and my children are with me in bed; I cannot rise and give thee. I say unto you, Though he will not rise and give him, because he is his friend, yet because of his importunity he will rise and give him as many as he needeth.*
>
> Luke 11:5–8

This parable is often taught as saying that God is like this friend. When you come asking for what you need, He may respond with the equivalent of, "I'm in bed. My children are in bed. I'm already asleep. Don't bother Me!" So you just have to keep petitioning, badgering, and staying after Him. You have to give God no rest and make Him get up and give you what you want just to get rid of you. That's not what this passage of scripture is teaching.

This parable is a contrast, not a comparison. I've used contrasts before many times. I remember one fellow I was ministering to who had just recently received the baptism in the Holy Spirit. He was bedridden with a life-threatening illness and didn't know for sure that God wanted to heal him. After sharing God's Word with him for quite a while, he still wasn't persuaded. Struggling to convince this man of the truth, I glanced over at his wife kneeling down right beside the bed and asked, "Do you think that your wife would want you to suffer through all of this pain you're going through, and then die?"

Friend?

He answered, "Oh, no. My wife loves me too much. If there was anything she could do to heal me, she'd do it."

"You've probably had arguments and fights with your wife at different times."

"Yeah, but there's nothing I've done that would ever cause her to want me to go through this suffering and pain, and just die."

Then I said, "And you think your wife—an imperfect human being—loves you more than Almighty God!"

That stopped his argument dead in its tracks.

God is love.

1 John 4:8

God—who is perfect—loves you infinitely more than any imperfect physical person does. That's the point Jesus was trying to get across. He asked, "How many of you have a friend...?" He wasn't talking about just an acquaintance—somebody you know—but rather someone you would call a friend. If you had a need at midnight and you called a friend on the phone, saying, "My car broke down. Could you help me?" do you have a friend who would say, "I'm in bed. My kids are in bed. Who cares about you? Call somebody else!" Someone like that isn't a friend.

The Opposite

Jesus was saying, "Do you know anyone, whom you consider a friend, who would treat you that rudely? Of course not! No friend would treat you that way. Then how do you expect God to be like that? Why do you think that you just have to badger Him?"

This true teaching of this passage is actually opposite of the way it's traditionally been interpreted. This passage is saying that if you expect that much mercy and kindness from a physical human being, then how much more should you expect God to answer your prayer without having to badger Him? It's making a contrast, and the context proves it. Jesus continued:

I say unto you, Ask, and it shall be given you; seek, and ye shall find; knock, and it shall be opened unto you. For every one that asketh receiveth; and he that seeketh findeth; and to him that knock-eth it shall be opened. If a son shall ask bread of any of you that is a father, will he give him a stone? or if he ask a fish, will he for a fish give him a serpent? Or if he shall ask an egg, will he offer him a scorpion? If ye then, being evil, know how to give good gifts unto your children: how much more shall your heavenly Father give the Holy Spirit to them that ask him?

Luke 11:9–13

In context, do you see what Jesus is trying to do? He asked the people, "How many of you would treat your children so badly that if they asked for a piece of bread you would give them a stone? If they asked for an egg, you'd give them a scorpion? How many of you would treat your children that way?" Hopefully, nobody! If you would treat your children this way, there are agencies here in America that will prosecute you. It's wrong to treat kids that way. Well then, if we who are corrupted, sinful, who do things for our own pleasure and self-benefit are better than this, how could we ever think that Almighty God is less compassionate than we are, that we, His children, would have to badger Him? We think that God won't respond to one person who asks for the power of God to be manifest, that we have to get a hundred million people together to manipulate, badger, and force Him into sending revival. There are some seriously wrong attitudes in the body of Christ today. We need to understand the balance of grace and faith.

Confident and Consistent

God, by grace, has anticipated the needs of the entire human race as well as every one of us individually. He's met every need that you will ever have. Before you ever had the problem, God had already created the answer. He made the supply before you ever had the need.

God has already provided everything. There's nothing that will ever come into your life that will catch God by surprise. You don't have to go to Him, begging for help and saying, "Oh God, I don't know if You can pull this off." The Lord has already dealt with everything.

Everything is already provided, but that doesn't mean you'll experience that provision unless you have an appropriate response of faith. Instead of panicking and becoming fearful, you must learn to trust in what He's done, resting and saying, "Father, I don't care what the doctor says. I know what You've said, and I trust You. I believe that You've already provided everything I need." Once you get this attitude and start living it, it creates in you such a sense of peace. You know that nothing will ever happen to you that God hadn't already anticipated. The supply was there before the need is. You will have such confidence that you don't have to be afraid of what the devil throws at you. It doesn't matter because God has already provided. That's faith.

Faith gives you consistency. Are you an up and down kind of Christian? Are you up as long as everything is wonderful and then when tragedy hits, you go into the valley? While in the valley, do you get desperate and start seeking God, begging and pleading until He comes through and you're back up again? If that's you, you're a very carnal person. You aren't resting in God. You are just living according to what you observe in the physical, natural realm. You don't understand that God, by grace, has already provided everything. Understanding this truth gives you consistency. It allows you to be the same at all times because God is the same at all times. Even though my finances, health, joy, and other circumstances may fluctuate, God's supply is the same. I'm able to just be consistent. I'm not afraid of any bad news because I know that God has already met the needs. I don't have to do something to force God to respond. That's good news!

Very few Christians have this attitude because very few understand that we're saved by grace through faith. They either emphasize grace to the point that they are just passive, refusing to take their authority and letting the devil beat them up because they have misunderstood the sovereignty of God, or they so emphasize faith that they are forever fasting, badgering God, trying to twist His arm to force Him to do something. In a sense, they have become "god" themselves, and are taking responsibility for making everything happen. Either situation is very frustrating.

Directing Angels

There are scriptures that talk about angels and how they work for us. (Matt. 18:10; Heb. 1:14.) In light of these scriptures, some people teach that you have to tell your angels where to go and what to do. You must command them to protect you when you get on that plane, train, or bus. You must station an angel on every corner of your car to protect you. The Word states that the angels behold the face of God. They aren't listening to you.

But the devil is listening to what you're saying. If, in your attempt to station your angels, you confess, "If anybody is going to have a wreck, it'll be me," Satan will take advantage of those words and you'll have what you say. It's fine to declare, "I'm blessed, I'm protected, and angels are watching over me." That's fine, but keep in mind the angels are beholding the face of God. They aren't listening for your guidance.

You aren't sharp enough to tell your angels what to do. There are so many things that go on in our life that we don't even know are happening. Once we get to heaven, we'll find out that there were many times the devil tried to kill us and we didn't even know it because we were walking in joy and peace, believing and trusting God. God commanded the angels and the Lord protected us.

Angels are real and they protect us. There are angels right where you are, but God is the One who directs them and takes care of you. Many people think that they have to assign their angels and that their angels can't do anything without being told by them what to do. You make a very poor god. It would be much better to just trust God and let Him be the One to direct the angels. He can see what you can't see. The Lord can take care of things much, much better than what you ever could.

Real Effort

These truths are the foundation for basic Christianity. You could consider them Christianity 101. They're as foundational as you can get. But if you lay hold of these truths, they will really make a positive difference in your life.

If you think God is controlling everything and causing all the tragedies, illnesses, and heartbreaks, then there is no way that you're ever going to resist these things lest you find yourself resisting God. If you think that the Lord is responding to you and you're the one making God move by your great faith, you're wrong. You can't bear that kind of responsibility. You simply aren't capable of doing that.

God loves you more than you love yourself. God loves your family more than you love them. He wants you to succeed even more than you want to succeed yourself. God, by grace, has provided everything that is necessary for you to accomplish what He wants you to do. It's already been done. Now you must simply rest and trust that God has already provided everything you need. That sounds easy, but the hardest thing you'll ever do is rest.

You must labor to enter into rest. (Heb. 4:11.) That sounds contradictory on the surface, but it's exactly the truth. The hardest thing you'll ever do is get to where you trust that God has already done everything instead of thinking that something still needs to be done. It's challenging to control your tongue, actions, and anxiety. This takes effort. You'll have to get into God's Word and start taking control of your thoughts with true knowledge instead of what the world has to say. This will take some real effort.

Paul said:

I laboured more abundantly than they all: yet not I, but the grace of God which was with me.

1 Corinthians 15:10

God, by grace, has provided everything. But it takes effort on our part to trust and rest in the truth that God has already done it.

Chapter 9

Believe and Receive

We're saved by grace through faith. (Eph. 2:8.) Grace is what God does for us independent of us. His work has nothing to do with us or it wouldn't be grace. Therefore, you didn't earn it. You didn't merit it. God didn't respond to us. Rather, grace is something that is done by God before we ever have a problem. It's done independent of us—independent of anything we deserve.

That's a wonderful truth; however, some folks have taken this truth that God does things independent of us, not based on our worth or value, and they've gone to an extreme. They forget that it takes faith on our part to release the grace of God.

Other people forget that it's God who provides everything. They actually think that we, by our faith, can make God move. They think that we can manipulate and force the Lord to do things, which is equally wrong.

We aren't saved by faith alone. Neither are we saved by grace alone. Both of these are poison by themselves. They must be taken together properly. We're saved by grace through faith.

True Biblical Faith

Everyone deals with the problem of understanding, "What is God's part, and what is my part? What does God do, and what must I do?" Probably one of the most common questions people ask me is, "What does God want me to do?" He wants you to understand, believe, and receive what He's already provided.

Faith isn't something you do, and then God responds to you. If you hold to this concept in any form or fashion, you think that God is looking at your Bible study, prayer, holiness, and goodness. You think that when you do enough, He'll release His power. If that's what you think, you aren't operating in true biblical faith. That thinking is legalistic and religious, and it's the reason that things aren't working in your life. Faith is not something you do to get God to do something. Faith is just your positive response to what God has already accomplished by grace. It's how you appropriate and receive what God has already provided.

God doesn't "move" when you believe Him. If you believe God for healing, He doesn't respond to you and heal you. First Peter 2:24 reveals that by His stripes, you were healed two thousand years ago.

...by [His] stripes ye were healed.

This is speaking of what happened in Herod's judgment hall. The Lord Jesus Christ, on His way to the cross, took those stripes on His back. (Matt. 27:26.) Jesus isn't healing people today. He healed people two thousand years ago. All of the power that it takes to heal every sickness, infirmity, and disease of the entire human race was generated two thousand years ago.

Raising-from-the-Dead Power

The very instant you received the Lord and became born again, God placed that raising-from-the-dead power on the inside of you. (Eph. 1:19.) You don't need God to heal you. He has already done it. He's placed raising-from-the-dead power on the inside of you in your born-again spirit. You just need to understand what has already been provided by grace and learn how to release that provision out into your soul and body by faith.

When the Lord showed me this truth, it transformed my life. These aren't things that I've just studied and made a message out of. This is what God has done in my life. This is how I live. It's how I think. I haven't arrived and I'm not perfect, but I've seen some super- natural things happen, including seeing my own son raised up after being dead for five hours.

In a meeting my team and I ministered in one evening, a lady received healing for a lump in her breast. The lump dissolved instantly. She went and checked herself. It was gone. In another meeting earlier that day, we ministered to several people who had pain, some for fifteen to twenty years. The pain left, instantly. They were healed. We have seen people healed of back problems, sinus problems, and many other things. I'm not saying that I have it all figured out, but I know I'm moving in the right direction. I'm seeing results that are beyond human explanation.

My life was transformed when I quit trying to get God to do something and started believing what He had already done instead. I began putting faith in grace instead of faith in my ability to make God move. This is where many people are missing the mark.

Paradigm Shift

When my eldest son was very young, he became sick with a certain illness on the same day in December every year. It didn't make any sense. I don't believe it was a physical problem, I believe it was a demonic attack. Just like clockwork, the same day every year he would get this same sickness.

After a few years of this, I began to anticipate the surely coming sickness. When I recognized the symptoms coming on my son again, I started fasting and praying, rebuking and binding, and many other things. But Joshua kept getting worse and worse. I remember praying, "God, I know this isn't right. I know this isn't normal. People don't get the same sickness on the same day every year. This is just the devil. Why is it that we aren't seeing better results?"

What the Lord said in response really changed my life. He said, "The problem is, you aren't fighting because I have healed you, you're trying to get healed. You see yourself as the sick trying to get well instead of the well from whom Satan is trying to steal your health."

From that point on, I made a paradigm shift and declared, "This is wrong. God has already healed us. By His stripes we were healed. He's already put this power on the inside of me and I'm acting like I'm the one who is fighting to obtain a victory. I already have the victory. I'm not fighting toward a victory. I'm coming from a victory. I have already been made more than a conqueror."

When you think that healing is over there and in the name of Jesus you are going to get there, you're in doubt. Even though this sounds positive, you're actually believing, "I'm not there." And if you're not there, then there is a possibility that you might not get there. But if you said, "I'm already healed. I refuse to let anybody take from me what God has already given me," how can you not get what you've already got? How can you not get there if you're already there?

Complete in Christ

I no longer see myself as the sick person who is trying to get well. I am a well person. God placed His power on the inside of me, and I'm not trying to get God to move.

Once you understand this foundational truth, it'll change your whole perspective. You'll see that the Christian life isn't about getting God to do anything. It's about renewing your mind to the truth of God's Word and receiving the physical manifestation of what He's already done. However, most people view the Christian life as seven steps to get God to do this and three steps to make God do that. It's all about how to get God to do something, and how to make Him move.

If I were to come into most Pentecostal, Spirit-filled, Charismatic, or other churches of this type today preaching, "It's double-portion time. God is going to pour out twice as much of the Holy Spirit. Would you like more of God? Do you want God to do something new in your life?" I can get nearly 99 percent of the people to run forward because they are looking for something. They're looking for God to do something new and touch them. Technically, all of that is wrong. God has already done everything that He's going to do.

On the inside of every born-again believer is the same power that raised Christ from the dead. The fullness of the Godhead dwells in you bodily. (Col. 1:27; 2:9.) You don't need God to do anything. You don't need God to bless you. You don't need joy or peace. You are complete in Christ. (Col. 2:10.)

Yet, you may still be struggling, thinking, *Well, you don't know me. I'm depressed.* That's because you're only looking on the outside. You're searching your emotions. Most of us don't understand what we have in our born-again spirit. In your spirit, you already have love, joy, peace, longsuffering, gentleness, goodness, faith, meekness, and temperance. (Gal. 5:22–23.) Those aren't things that are "out there," and if you'll pray hard enough, study the Word, live holy, and do right, then God will give you love, joy, and peace. No, in your spirit, twenty-four hours a day, seven days a week, every day of your life, your born-again spirit is rejoicing and praising God. It has never been depressed. It is never discouraged. When you're depressed and saying,

"Oh God, where are You? It feels like You just up and left," it's never your spirit voicing these things. That's only your flesh speaking because you are going by what you can see and feel. But there is a spiritual part of you that is seated with Christ Jesus in heavenly places. (Eph. 1:3; Col. 3:1.)

God Is Always On

The truth is, if you're a born-again believer, you already have the same power on the inside of you that raised Jesus Christ from the dead. You have more than enough healing. You don't need God to heal you, you need to find out what He's already provided. Once you get this revelation, it'll change your entire mind-set. Instead of trying to get healed, you'll know God has healed you and you'll defend what God has already given you. You're not going to let the devil steal it from you. This makes all the difference in the world!

When the Lord revealed this truth to me, I had been fighting this sickness that, for years, attacked my son on the same day every year. I'd fight the sickness and eventually, I'd see him get healed. It looked like we were going to go through this thing again, but once the Lord showed me this truth, in ten minutes time the sickness was over and that was the end of that. Why? I was no longer trying to get my son healed. I knew he was already healed and there wasn't a devil big enough to steal from me what God had already given me. It's much easier to defend what you've already got than it is to try and get something that you don't have.

When people come up to me and ask, "Would you please pray that God would pour out His love in my life?" the spirit of slap just comes all over me. What they're implying is that God, for whatever reason, has shut off the flow of His love, peace, joy, or whatever. They think that the reason they don't feel love, peace, or joy is because God hasn't released it. That's never true!

Grace is independent of you, and it's consistent. That means it isn't based on you. It's not based on whether you've lived a holy life or done anything right or wrong. His grace is always the same. The grace of God never fluctuates or changes. The Lord never releases His power into your life, and then when you do something wrong, switches it off. Religion teaches that, but the truth is God is always on. He's always releasing His power.

Take Revival

I'm definitely for revival, but the way most of the body of Christ seeks revival is wrong. The Lord isn't up in heaven with His arms folded, saying, "I'm not sending revival until more people pray longer and harder, until you get another 100,000 people together, until you beg, plead, and repent some more…." This implies that God controls revival and it's just up to Him to "send" it. This attitude says that if God wanted us to, we could be having red-hot revival. All of our churches would be packed out and our entire nation would be turning to God. In essence it is saying that God is our problem. He's the One not sending revival.

It's not like that at all. God's arms aren't folded—they're wide open. He's trying to release His power through us. God wants us to be revived much more than we do. We don't need to plead with Him. We just need to start believing that He's already placed revival on the inside of us. We already have the same power that raised Christ from the dead, and we can do the same works that Jesus did. Just go out and raise a few people from the dead. You'll have all the revival you can handle!

We're praying, "Oh God, send revival," but He's saying, "You go take revival. I've already placed My power on the inside of you—release it!" Most of the Church is wondering why God hasn't moved, why He hasn't done something. God has already done everything. He moved through the death, burial, and resurrection of the Lord Jesus Christ. Everything that God will ever do for the whole human race has already been accomplished through the atonement. It's done. When Jesus said, "It is finished," it was finished. He accomplished it. It was done. You don't need God to save you or heal you. He's already saved and healed you. He's forgiven the sins of the whole world and provided healing. God's grace has already provided, the issue is: Will you believe and receive, or doubt and do without?

God, by grace, has already moved. He's already done everything He'll ever do. Through Christ's atonement, He's already provided everything we'll ever need. Now it's just up to us to appropriate—receive—it by faith.

Chapter 10
Turn On and Tune In

Blessed be the God and Father of our Lord Jesus Christ, who hath [past tense] *blessed us...*

Ephesians 1:3

The word "hath" in this verse means it's already been done. We're already blessed. It doesn't say, "Who is going to [future tense]...." Most prophecies in the body of Christ today focus on the future. They say, "God is going to do this, and God is going to do that. He's going to move and do something new!" The Lord is presented as the great "I'm going to be," not the great I Am. The average prophecy today says, "There's something coming, but right now there's nothing." Yet, this isn't the message of the Bible. Here in Ephesians 1:3, the Word reveals that we're already blessed. The whole book of Ephesians was written from this perspective that it's already done. God has already...

...blessed us with all spiritual blessings in heavenly places in Christ.

Ephesians 1:3

This is just an old English way of saying that He's given us all earthly and spiritual blessings—and they're already in us in Christ. God has already deposited everything we'll ever need into our born-again spirit. It's already done. God has already passed His blessings out.

Therefore, it's an act of unbelief to pray, "Oh God, bless me." You're already blessed. You just haven't heard God's Word, believed the truth, and seen it manifested yet. God has already commanded the blessing upon you, but you just haven't received it yet.

You Were Healed

It's an insult to God to pray, "Oh God, heal me." First Peter 2:24 says:

By whose stripes ye were [past tense] *healed.*

If God says, "You were healed," and then you say, "Oh God, heal me," one of you is wrong. Let me just suggest to you that it isn't God who's wrong. He says, by His stripes you were healed. If you *were* healed, then you *are* healed. Why are you asking God to do something that He's already done?

"But I have a doctor's report and pain in my body that proves I'm not healed." No, that just proves that your physical body hasn't yet received the healing that God has already given. According to the scriptures, God has already healed you. The resurrection power He's placed within you is certainly enough to heal your hangnail, cold, headache, cancer, or AIDS. None of these things are a problem for God. He has already placed supernatural healing power on the inside of you, yet you're still asking Him for it. That's unbelief.

How do you think I would respond if I gave you my Bible, but then you walked up to me and asked, "Andrew, would you please give me your Bible so I could look up a scripture?" How do you respond when a person asks you to give them something that you know you've already given to them? Personally, I don't even know how I would respond. I'd probably just look at them like, "What's wrong?"

If God could be confused, I believe that He would be by our unbelief. All these millions of people are praying, "Oh God, please heal me. Stretch forth Your hand and heal. I'm believing You to come and heal me."

Already Anointed

They also pray, "Oh God, rend the heavens and come down." You may be thinking, *That's in the Bible. What's wrong with that?* God already rent the heavens and came down through Jesus. It was appropriate for Isaiah to pray, "Rend the heavens and come down" because God hadn't done it yet. (Isa. 64:1.) However, it's inappropriate to pray this way on this side of the life, death, and resurrection of the Lord Jesus Christ. People who pray this way aren't valuing Jesus properly. They're basically saying, "I know Jesus came down, but what He did isn't enough. I need God to do something else!"

Before Jesus came, it was appropriate for David to pray:

> *Create in me a clean heart, O God; and renew a right spirit within me. Cast me not away from thy presence; and take not thy holy spirit from me. Restore unto me the joy of thy salvation; and uphold me with thy free spirit.*
>
> Psalm 51:10–12

But it's unbelief for a Christian to pray this way today. David was an Old Testament man who wasn't born again. He didn't have the promises we do which say, "I will never leave thee, nor forsake thee" (Heb. 13:5) and "I am with you alway even unto the end of the world" (Matt. 28:20). It's unbelief for us to come into a church service and pray, "Oh God, we ask You to meet with us today." In addition to the promise we have in Hebrews 13:5 that He will never leave us, nor forsake us, Jesus said:

> For where two or three are gathered together in my name, there am I in the midst of them.
>
> Matthew 18:20

We don't have to pray and ask for the anointing to fall. God has already anointed us. When Jesus came into His hometown of Nazareth, He stood up and quoted from Isaiah 61 saying:

> The Spirit of the Lord is upon me, because he hath anointed me to preach the gospel to the poor.
>
> Luke 4:18

He didn't go into a back room with the preacher and say, "Let's pray and ask God to anoint you." People do this with me all the time when I go to their church. They ask, "Would you like to come back here with us? We want to pray for God to anoint you." I am so polite, kind, and non-confrontational that I usually don't say anything, but what is the point of asking God to anoint me? If I don't have the anointing of God by the time I get to your church to minister, I'm not going to get it in the next five minutes. If you don't believe that I'm anointed and that God speaks through me, why would you invite me to your church in the first place? Why go in the back room and spend thirty minutes praying and asking for God's anointing? It's unbelief. Desiring to see the power of God in manifestation is good, but you don't have to beg God for the anointing.

Agree with God's Word

If God tells us to do something, He would be unjust not to give us what we need to do it. Naturally speaking, I'm an introvert. As a teenager, I couldn't even look someone else in the face. Yet God has called me to speak to millions of people worldwide every day through television, radio, and Internet. He's called me to hold conferences and citywide meetings, and to minister in churches and Bible schools. God would be unjust to tell me to do something that I can't do and not supply me with everything I need to do it. He doesn't just command us and then turn us loose on our own until we beg Him for help. No, anything God tells us to do, there is an anointing present to get it accomplished.

You don't have to beg God for the anointing. Actually, by approaching Him and saying, "Oh God, please anoint me," you're praying from a position of unbelief. You're saying that you aren't anointed when the scripture says that God...

...hath anointed us...

2 Corinthians 1:21

I'm already anointed. You're anointed. (1 John 2:20.) God has anointed every one of his children. So instead of praying in unbelief, saying, "Oh God, I'm not anointed, but would You anoint me?" you need to start believing that He has already anointed you (2 Cor. 1:21) and has blessed you with all spiritual blessings (Eph. 1:3). Agree with God's Word, declaring, "I've already been blessed. I already have love, joy, and peace. I don't need God to give it to me. If I don't feel joy, it's not because God hasn't given it to me. Somehow or another I have switched off the joy of the Lord. What I need to do is work on my receiver, not God's transmitter."

Right now, there are television signals wherever you are. You may not believe this to be true, but your unbelief doesn't mean the signals aren't there. It just means that you aren't very smart. You say, "But I can't see or hear them." That doesn't mean they aren't there. They're there. They're just in a form that you can't perceive with your natural senses.

If you plug in, turn on, and tune in a television set, you'd start seeing and hearing the program, but that's not when the signal started. The signal was already there. It's being broadcast twenty-four hours a day, seven days a week. In fact, there are multiple signals—both television and radio—all around you. There are all kinds of things happening in the unseen realm all around you. You may not be perceiving them, but they're there. The station doesn't start broadcasting when you turn on and tune in your television set; that's just when you start receiving.

What About Daniel?

God is always releasing—broadcasting—love, joy, peace, longsuffering, gentleness, and goodness. And it's not coming from "out there" somewhere.

We don't have to clear a hole through the demonic powers over our city so that our prayers can get through to God, as some people might think. No, that's just a religious doctrine. "Then what about Daniel?" someone might ask. Daniel was an Old Testament man. Jesus hadn't yet died and broken the dominion of the devil.

In the New Covenant, you don't need your prayers to get above the ceiling. You don't even need them to get above your nose. God lives on the inside of you. The reason you bow your head to pray is so you can look at God. Believing this erroneous concept that demons are blocking your prayers from getting up to God shows that you don't understand what the Lord has already done through grace. That's the reason Satan is eating your lunch and popping the bag—you're lacking important knowledge. (Hos. 4:6.)

You feel too desperate to have a move from God. God has already moved through Jesus, and He's placed on the inside of you the same power that raised Christ from the dead. You can go out and do the same works that Jesus did. Start representing Him truthfully as somebody who has done everything. Quit representing the Lord as someone who could move if we pray hard enough. Go out and proclaim, "Good news! God has already done it. He's already provided everything you need. He's already forgiven your sins. He's already healed you. Will you believe and receive?"

That's a much different approach than saying, "Let's pray and ask God to move." If we would represent God correctly, we'd see much better results. Let's stop begging the Lord to do something and start acting like He's already done it. When we start believing His Word and releasing His power, we'll have more revival than we can handle.

Check Your Receiver

Unfortunately for most Christians, their tuner isn't working. And instead of checking to see if they're plugged in, turning the power on, or seeing if they have the channel adjusted, the first thing they do is call the broadcasting station. "Why aren't you transmitting? Please turn on the power and start sending a signal. I want to watch Andrew's program!"

The first thing we do if we have sickness in our body is say, "God, why haven't You healed me?" God is broadcasting healing 24/7. If you aren't receiving healing, it's not God who hasn't released it. It's you who don't know how to receive it. I'm not saying this to condemn you. It takes time to get educated and learn. But you must start by recognizing that God is not the One who hasn't healed anybody. He has already healed all of our sicknesses and diseases and that power is already on the inside of us. If we aren't feeling it—if it isn't manifest—it's not God who hasn't given. It's us who haven't learned to receive. We need to start working on our receiver, not questioning God's transmitter.

Don't call the station and say, "God, what's wrong with You? Broadcast! Oh God, pour out Your power. Oh Lord, send revival!" God is not our problem. He's been releasing His power for over two thousand years now. The reason why the church suffers isn't that God hasn't been moving. It's that we haven't been receiving. We've been ignorant, and Satan has been stealing from us.

Chapter 11

Open Your Eyes

If you were writing a prayer that would be read by and prayed for the saints two thousand years in the future, how would you pray? Think about that for a moment.

The exact wording might vary, but the typical Christian today would pray something like, "Oh God, we ask You to pour out Your power on this generation. Just move and send revival. Oh God, we ask for a new...." It would all be some form of pleading with God to do a new thing, to move, to do something.

Let's take a look at the way Paul approached this task in Ephesians 1:15–23. The only thing he asked God to do is give us a revelation of what the Lord had already done. Paul didn't ask God to do anything new. He just said, "Open up their eyes to what You've already done." He was praying for every believer to receive revelation of what they already have.

Spirit and Life

I won't pray for someone who comes up to me and asks, "Will you please pray that God will pour out His love in my life?" because God has already poured out His love through Jesus. He sent the Holy Spirit who shed abroad the love of God in our hearts. (Rom. 5:5.) There is no problem with God's love. He loves every one of us infinitely more than any of us have ever understood. We don't need God to pour out His love.

However, if you ask, "Would you please pray with me to receive a revelation of what I know is true. I know God loves me, but I don't have a revelation of it. I don't understand it, and I'm not walking in it." I'll pray with you in a heartbeat for that. I'm happy to help you fix your receiver, but I refuse to impute to God that He doesn't love you. God loves you.

You may complain that you don't feel the love of God. Well then, your feelings are wrong. They're broken. But it's not God who isn't transmitting His love. You may say that you don't feel the joy of the Lord or His peace. Your feelings are wrong because the truth is you have love, joy, and peace on the inside of you all of the time.

Every time you've been depressed and discouraged, your spirit is just rejoicing and praising God. Your spirit is always happy and blessed. You may be thinking, *No, it's not. I would know if it was.* That's not true. That which is spirit is spirit, and that which is flesh is flesh. (John 3:6.) You can't tell what's going on in the spirit realm unless you get into the Word of God.

The words that I speak unto you, they are spirit, and they are life.

John 6:63

"Thank You, Father"

Let's read Paul's prayer in Ephesians 1:15–16.

Wherefore I also, after I heard of your faith in the Lord Jesus, and love unto all the saints, cease not to give thanks for you, making mention of you in my prayers.

In our prayers, not many of us give thanks. Our prayers consist of, "Oh God, I need this. Please give me that. Oh God, help me…forgive me." That's what most people's prayers are about. If you are a spiritual giant today, then your prayer is all about "Oh God, give them this, and give them that. Oh God, forgive them." Notice that 99.9 percent of all prayer is about your needs. There's not a lot of thanksgiving and praise because again, we don't see God as having done much. We see Him as able to do anything, but He hasn't done very much. We feel we must constantly petition Him. However, once you start understanding that by grace it's already been done, then your prayers turn more toward thanksgiving.

I don't sit down and consciously evaluate my prayers, but I guarantee you that 95 to 99 percent of my prayers are prayers of thanksgiving and expressing my love to God. I spend virtually no time asking God for anything because He's already provided it.

You may be thinking that I'm weird. Well, if you are one of those people who are always praying about your needs, then I think you're weird, and until you start getting better results than I am, maybe you ought to consider doing it the way I am.

Enlightened

Paul was praying in Ephesians 1:16–17, I...

Cease not to give thanks for you, making mention of you in my prayers; that the God of our Lord Jesus Christ, the Father of glory, may give unto you the spirit of wisdom and revelation in the knowledge of him.

For the sake of accuracy, verses 8 and 9 say that God has already...

...abounded toward us in all wisdom and prudence; having made known unto us the mystery of his will...

The truth is God has already given us wisdom and prudence, making known to us the mystery of His will. In verses 16 and 17, Paul was just praying that this wisdom and prudence will start functioning in our lives. He's not asking God to do something that He hasn't done. He's praying that we'd understand what the Lord has already given us.

The eyes of your understanding being enlightened; that ye may know what is the hope of his calling, and what the riches of the glory of his inheritance in the saints.

Ephesians 1:18

He's praying that your eyes would be opened—not your physical eyes, but your spiritual eyes. He's talking about the eyes of your heart.

Sixth Sense

Personally, I believe that God originally created us with six senses, not five. We walked by faith. Adam and Eve communicated with God through the spirit. When Genesis 3:7 says that their eyes were opened, it isn't talking about the eyes of their heart. It was talking about their physical eyesight which began to dominate them. They were created with a sixth sense of faith, which they originally walked by. But once they fell, their spiritual eyes became closed and their physical eyes opened up to the existence that most of us live in now. We're carnal, and we just go by what we see. We don't have any spiritual perception at all. Originally, God made man to be able to perceive things in the spirit realm.

In 2 Kings 6, there's an instance where Elisha was surrounded with a Syrian host. His servant exclaimed:

Alas, my master! how shall we do?

2 Kings 6:15

Elisha prayed and said, "Lord, open up the young man's eyes" (v. 17). He wasn't talking about his physical eyes. His physical eyes were already as big as saucers looking at all of the enemy troops round about them. Elisha was praying that his servant's spiritual eyes would be opened. All of a sudden, this young man saw with his heart and perceived all the defending angels.

Adam and Eve could see into the spirit realm because they were walking by faith through the eyes of their heart until the fall. This instance in 2 Kings 6 is the exact opposite of what happened with Adam and Eve. Adam and Eve degenerated from seeing and walking by faith to seeing and walking by sight. Elisha's servant went from seeing by sight to seeing by faith and perceiving the spirit realm.

Now, through the new birth...

We walk by faith, not by sight.

2 Corinthians 5:7

The norm for the New Testament believer should be walking by faith. We should have this sixth sense of faith restored to where we can see things with our hearts that we can't see with our physical eyes. That's normal.

Supernatural

In Ephesians 1:17–18, Paul was praying that our spiritual eyesight—our spiritual understanding—would begin to perceive things that we can't perceive with our natural senses. He prays that through the eyes of our heart, we would start to perceive...

...the hope of his calling...

Ephesians 1:18

This isn't just the hope of *your* calling. It's the hope of *His* calling!

Now that you're born again, you have a calling that is beyond human ability. Most people are trying to find out what God wants them to do; however, they are looking for something that they are capable of doing on their own. They pray, "God, show me what You want me to do." If what you feel God called you to do is something that you can accomplish yourself, then you haven't truly found God's will for your life yet. God has a plan for you that is supernatural. It's going to take His supernatural ability working through you to do it.

I was an introvert and couldn't look a person in the face. Now God has me speaking to thousands and thousands of people. I'm doing something that is impossible for me to do on my own.

If you can do something on your own, I doubt if it's God's call. He will call you to something that is supernatural. This is the hope of His calling. God is a supernatural God, and most of us are shooting way too low. We're aiming at nothing, and hitting it every time. We need to increase our perspective. We need to get our eyes opened and our understanding enlightened so we can see the hope of His calling—what God's plan is for you, something far bigger than what you think you can accomplish on your own.

In the Saints

The eyes of your understanding being enlightened; that ye may know what is...the riches of the glory of his inheritance in the saints.

Ephesians 1:18

Notice how the Word says that we would see what is (present tense) the riches of the glory of His inheritance *in* the saints. His inheritance is in the saints.

We sing these songs about when we all get to heaven what a day that will be. In the sweet by and by it will be wonderful, but in the rough here and now it's a drag. But the Word says that we have been called…

> …*to the obtaining of the glory of our Lord Jesus Christ.*
>
> 2 Thessalonians 2:14

We have already obtained the glory of the Lord Jesus Christ. You may be saying, "I don't understand that." You go look in the mirror and think, *This is glory?* No, the Word isn't talking about your physical body or your soul (mental and emotional realm). But in the spirit, you are full of the glory of God. If what's on the inside of your born-again spirit had to be replaced, it would bankrupt heaven to put back inside you what you already have. The glory of God dwells inside you. The riches of the glory of His inheritance is in the saints. It's not out there somewhere. It's already on the inside of you.

Most Christians don't know that God has already placed this inside of us. We think that when we all get to heaven, what a day that will be. But really, all that will happen in heaven is you'll get a full revelation of what you already have. That's the reason God will have to wipe tears away from our eyes. It's not because we came through such terrible things, barely got into heaven, and so we're weeping and wailing until He wipes our tears away. No, we will weep when we stand before God and finally recognize what we had all along.

For I reckon that the sufferings of this present time are not worthy to be compared with the glory which shall be revealed in us.

Romans 8:18

Not *to* us, but *in* us! One day we will stand before God and suddenly know all things even as also we are known. (1 Cor. 13:12.) We'll say, "God, You mean that whole time I had the same power on the inside of me that raised Jesus from the dead? I could have been raising the dead, solving problems, and walking in joy, peace, and victory all along?" We'll be crying and saying, "Oh God. I missed it!" He'll have to wipe the tears away from our eyes and supernaturally enable us to enjoy heaven once we find out how we let the devil beat us down and destroy us in this life. The riches of the glory of His inheritance is in the saints.

Chapter 12
The Same Power

In Ephesians 1:19–21, Paul prayed that we would get a revelation of...

> *What is the exceeding greatness of his power to us-ward who believe, according to* [to the proportion of or to the degree of] *the working of his mighty power, which he wrought in Christ, when he raised him from the dead, and set him at his own right hand in the heavenly places, far above all principality, and power, and might, and dominion, and every name that is named, not only in this world, but also in that which is to come.*

He was praying that God would show us the exceeding greatness of His power that is already on the inside of us. It's the same power that He used when He raised Jesus from the dead.

Again, Ephesians 1:3 reveals that God "hath" already blessed us with these things. Paul wasn't praying that the Lord will give us this power, that He'll release more power, or that we'll get a double portion of the Holy Spirit. He was praying that we would receive a revelation of what God has already put on the inside of us.

The power that is on the inside of every born-again believer is the exact same power God used when He raised Jesus from the dead. Satan mustered every ounce of strength he had to oppose the resurrection. He put all of his power, every one of his demonic forces, right in front of that tomb trying to block Jesus from coming out. Yet the power that raised Christ from the dead was much greater than all the force of the enemy. And now, as a born-again believer, you have that same power on the inside of you. That's awesome!

"Real Dumb"

I like the way the mega-church my wife and I attend dramatizes this truth at the annual Easter presentation. As they trace the story of Jesus, one actor dresses in black and plays the part of Satan. Among other places, he shows up in the desert to tempt the Lord and in the crowd before Pilate yelling, "Crucify Him, crucify Him!" When it comes to the resurrection scene, the devil stands there pushing on the tombstone, trying to keep Jesus from resurrecting, then there's a huge explosion. Once the smoke finally clears, Jesus is standing on top of the tombstone, which is lying on top of Satan.

The devil gave it everything he had, but Jesus rose from the dead and overcame all the power of the enemy. Yet many Christians are saying, "Oh God, could You please heal me? Could You please spare just enough power to make me well?"

A guy walked up to me once and said, "I have a sore neck, my back hurts, and I have sciatica all the way down my leg so that my feet are numb. I have neuropathy…," and he started naming all sorts of other ailments. I just listened to him. Then he looked at me and said, "But do you know what? I could live with the rest if God would just heal the pain that's in my back and neck."

I answered, "Oh, I understand what you're saying. If we were to ask God to heal your neck, back, nerves, feet—everything—the lights in heaven might dim. I'm not sure God could pull all that off at once. Let's not ask Him for very much."

This guy looked at me and said, "What I said was kind of dumb, wasn't it?"

I said, "Yes, it was. Real dumb."

That's the way many people approach God. They say, "Oh God, I'm just asking this little bit of You. Could You please spare enough power to do this?" As a born-again believer, you have the same power on the inside of you that raised Jesus from the dead. That is greater than the power it took to create the universe. Raising Jesus from the dead is the greatest display of God's power in the history of the universe. Yet here we are saying, "Oh God, could You heal a cold?" I've had people come up to me asking, "Can God heal AIDS?" That just expresses how full of unbelief we are.

Flip the Switch

You have the same power on the inside of you that raised Jesus Christ from the dead. All things are possible with God. It's not the Lord who is out there turning the power switch on and off. He's placed His generator—His power—on the inside of you. If you aren't seeing the power of God, it's not because God hasn't given you His power. It's because you haven't flipped the switch. You haven't turned on and released His power. God has already done it. By grace it's already been provided.

Now are you going to reach out in faith and partake of what God has provided, or will you keep asking God as if He hasn't done anything? Are you going to continue in unbelief saying, "Oh God, would You please move in my life?" when the Bible reveals that He's already moved? Are you going to ask God to rend the heavens, not believing that He has already rent the heavens and come down through Jesus? Are you going to ask Him to heal you when He says that by His stripes you were healed? Are you going to ask Him to give you joy and peace and pour out His love in your life when the Word says that you already have the fruit of the Spirit—love, joy, and peace? It's already on the inside of you—and that's good news!

When I minister these truths, people usually wonder, *Well then, what do we pray?* I'm glad you asked! The vast majority of the body of Christ prays nothing but unbelief, which is the reason their prayers are not yielding results. I know this issue is a sacred cow. I'm aware this teaching is offensive to some people, but the vast majority of Christians aren't pleased with the results they're getting from their prayers. Yet, they become offended if someone suggests to them that they aren't praying correctly. They want to keep doing the same thing, but expect different results. That's insane. If what you're doing isn't working, you ought to consider that maybe you're doing something wrong. Your prayers would be much more effective if you just began thanking God for what He's already done instead of asking Him to do something that He hasn't. It takes faith to thank God.

If you're believing for healing, but you haven't seen or felt the manifestation yet, start thanking and praising God. Colossians 2:7 reveals that faith abounds with thanksgiving. If you would start thanking God, your faith would rise up and all of a sudden things would start happening. It's much easier to say, "Oh Father, thank You, thank You, thank You that You've already done it." If you spend enough time meditating and thanking God for what He's done, you'll start believing that He's done it. And the moment you believe it, grace and faith together will release the supernatural power of God and you'll experience in your body what God has already provided.

Sister Goiter

At a certain charismatic ministers' conference, a woman who had a big goiter on her neck came forward and received prayer. After prayer, she knew that she knew that she knew that God had healed her. So she stood up in front of this large group of people and began to praise God that He had healed her, even though she still had this big goiter on her neck. The people praised God with her and thanked her for her testimony, believing that the healing power of God was there, working, and would manifest itself. The people at this conference gave this woman mercy and grace even though they couldn't yet see any visible results.

The next year she returned to that same conference, stood up, and testified, saying, "Tonight is the one-year anniversary of when Jesus healed my goiter." Yet, she still had this big goiter on her neck. This time, the people didn't rejoice. They didn't praise God because they thought something was wrong, but they let it pass.

The following year this woman came back and said, "This is the two-year anniversary of when God healed this goiter." People became upset and went to the conference leadership saying, "You must tell that woman to quit testifying because it's obvious that she's not healed. She's making a fool of herself and mocking the things of God. You need to tell her to quit!" So the leadership went and told this woman, "You can't testify anymore until that goiter is gone."

This woman went to the Lord that night and prayed, "God, I know that You healed me. I believe that You healed me that night I received prayer. I know it's been done. But these preachers can't believe unless they see it. Will You please take this thing away so that they can believe what You've already done?" The next morning when she woke up, the goiter was gone, and she testified, "I told you I was healed!"

Don't get me wrong. I'm not saying that we should just go around testifying about things that aren't manifest. However, I am saying that we need to get to that place where we believe what the Word says God has already done so strongly that whether we've experienced it yet in our body is immaterial. We know it's true.

Normal

I haven't arrived in this area, but I'm coming to a place where things I see on the inside are more real to me than what I see on the outside. It's true.

I remember being in a meeting once where I saw—in the spirit— the Lord walk into the room. Although my natural eyes were closed, what I saw with the eyes of my heart was so real. In fact, I opened up my natural eyes to see if I could see it. I could see everything that was happening as I saw it in my heart, except I couldn't see Jesus.

In my heart, I saw Jesus walk over to a woman and touch her, and she fell flat on her face. Then He walked over to another lady and she just knelt down and lifted up her hand. I saw the Lord start touching people one by one. When I opened up my eyes, I saw all of the physical things happening, but I couldn't see the Lord. In my heart, I could see the Lord. I could see these events happening before they happened in the natural. What I was seeing with my heart was more real, more vivid, and clearer than what I was seeing with my eyes. So eventually, I just closed my eyes because I could see better with my heart than I could with my natural eyes.

This should be normal, not abnormal. We should walk by faith, not by sight. (2 Cor. 5:7.) We can get to where we see what God has done for us by grace. Then we enter into it by faith and begin to rejoice. When you get to a place where you are so lost in what God has done and you are praising Him for it, then the physical realm will just reflect it nearly as a by-product. You'll get to a place where you can say, "God, I know I'm already healed, but wouldn't it be a great testimony to this doctor if they could see and prove it in a test tube?" You don't have to see it to believe. You want it manifest so that other people can see.

We're living far below our God-given privileges. We have an entirely wrong mind-set towards God. We believe He could do anything, but that He has done nothing, and we have to beg and plead with Him. There's a better way. Find out what God has already provided by grace and then just appropriate by faith what is already done. You don't have to labor to make it happen. That's awesome!

"Such As I Have"

This is the reason we can heal the sick. The Bible doesn't tell you to pray for the sick. Although James 5 mentions that if you're sick you should call for the church elders to come and pray for you, nowhere in the Bible are you commanded to *pray* for the sick. However, we are commanded to *heal* the sick.

> *Heal the sick, cleanse the lepers, raise the dead, cast out devils: freely ye have received, freely give.*
>
> Matthew 10:8

There's a huge difference between saying, "You're healed in Jesus' name. I release the healing power of God," and saying, "Dear Father, if it be Your will, for Jesus' sake, stretch forth Your hand and heal that person." That's a chicken prayer! It takes no faith to pray that. Nothing is on the line.

We need to stand up in faith and speak like Peter did when he entered the temple with John. To the lame beggar who asked for alms, Peter said, "I don't have any money with me right now. I left my wallet at home, but…"

> *Such as I have give I thee: In the name of Jesus Christ of Nazareth rise up and walk.*
>
> Acts 3:6

"Such as I have give I thee…," most people would kick these disciples out of their church, saying, "How dare you say that you have the healing power of God!"

The Difference

The Lord did say:

> *Without me ye can do nothing.*
>
> John 15:5

I, myself, am not the Healer. It's not my power I rely upon. On my own, I can't heal a gnat. But I'm not on my own. God said He would never leave me nor forsake me. (Heb. 13:5.) I have the healing power of God on the inside of me—the same power that raised Jesus from the dead. Because of that I can say with Peter, "Such as I have." I have the healing power of God and in the name of Jesus I can command healing in people. This is a completely different approach.

God has already provided everything by grace. Now we have to get into a position of faith. Instead of trying to believe that it's going to happen, we must believe it's a done deal. It's already been done. You've already got it, so quit trying to get it. Just operate in what God said He's already done. It's the difference between victory and defeat.

Chapter 13

Mix with Faith

Faith reaches out and appropriates what God has already provided for us by grace. We don't have to ask, beg, or plead with God. He's already supplied what we need. It's just a matter of us believing and receiving.

You may ask what the meaning is, then, of the scriptures that speak of asking:

> *This is the confidence that we have in him, that, if we ask any thing according to his will, he heareth us: And if we know that he hear us, whatsoever we ask, we know that we have the petitions that we desired of him.*

> 1 John 5:14–15

It's not wrong to ask. God has already provided everything, so technically you don't have to ask for it. Just believe and receive, command and release the power of God. The harmony between this is the attitude in which you ask.

A Polite Demand

Consider what Jesus said in what's commonly called "The Lord's Prayer."

> *After this manner therefore pray ye: Our Father which art in heaven, Hallowed be thy name. Thy kingdom come. Thy will be done in earth, as it is in heaven. Give us this day our daily bread.*
>
> Matthew 6:9–11

"Give us this day our daily bread" is a petition for God to meet your daily needs; however, it's not phrased as "Would You please give us this day our daily bread?" as if you are wondering if and will He do so. No, it's more of a demand. It's similar to a child saying to their mother at mealtime, "Can I have something to eat?"

What would you think if you were over at my house when my kids were little, and one of them came in, fell on their knees before me, put their hands together, and said, "Oh father, I'm so ungodly, and I know I don't deserve it, but would you please give me a piece of bread? Could I please have a morsel of food?" If they started begging me like that, you'd surely think that something was wrong in our home.

A child, if they're trained properly, doesn't just come in and say, "Give me something to eat!" That's wrong too. They might say, "Could I please have something to eat?" They're asking a question, but there's really no question involved. They know that you love them. They know that you're going to supply. So they are really placing a demand. They are just doing it in a polite, kind way.

I'm not saying that we don't ever acknowledge our need or make a request, saying, "God, I need You to supply something." However, it's not a begging request. It's not a request with a question mark at the end to indicate that you're doubting that God will provide. Your request is more just a polite way of coming to your Father and saying, "Father, I know that You've already provided all of my needs. I'm ready to receive Your provision. Can I have it now?"

Beggar or Believer?

It's not wrong to petition God in faith. But to throw a petition out there not knowing if God's going to answer it or not, feeling like you have to grovel in the dirt, begging and pleading, is a religious concept that's absolutely contrary to what the scriptures teach.

Imagine me walking up to you right now and saying, "After you finish reading this chapter, I'll give you the keys to my car. You can use it to go and do whatever you want." If I gave you that promise, then after finishing this chapter you would come up to me and say, "Can I have the keys to your car?" You could do that in a couple of different ways. You could be thinking, *Would Andrew really let me have his car? I don't believe that. I'm not sure it's true. Would he really do this?* In that case, you would come up to me and say, "Can I have the keys to your car?" like, "Is this really true? Would you really do this?" You're asking out of unbelief. Or you could say, "Can I have the keys to your car," in a tone reflecting that you believed my words completely, and then all you're saying is, "I'm ready now. You said it. Here I am requesting it. Can I have the keys to your car?"

You can say the exact same words, but with very different motives. You could be simply making your polite demand, trusting that what I said is true, or your words could be spoken in unbelief. It's the second scenario, this unbelief, that this teaching is meant to counter.

People pray, "Lord, if it be Your will, please touch me and move in my life." It is God's will. He's already supplied everything. Instead of approaching the Lord as a beggar, we need to be believers who trust His promises, and confidently and gratefully just take advantage of what He's already provided for us. That's a powerful truth!

Cautious, Aware, and Diligent

It was this attitude of unbelief that hindered the Jews from receiving God's provision and entering into the Promised Land.

> *So we see that they could not enter in because of unbelief.*
>
> Hebrews 3:19

Again, anyone who believes that God's will just automatically comes to pass has not been paying attention when they read the Bible. It wasn't God's will for the children of Israel to spend forty years in the wilderness after coming out from the land of Egypt. This happened because of their unbelief (Num. 13,14; Psa. 78:40–41). God's will did not come to pass because the children of Israel did not cooperate with God in faith. They didn't enter into the Promised Land. The generation that came out of Egypt died in the wilderness and never did see God's will for them come to pass because of their unbelief.

> *Let us therefore fear, lest, a promise being left us of entering into his rest, any of you should seem to come short of it.*
>
> Hebrews 4:1

This verse is useless to those who say that God sovereignly does everything and nothing happens but what is His will. Hebrews 4:1 is saying you need to be careful, cautious, and aware. You need to be diligent because you could miss God's will for you. This verse would be a useless statement if God just automatically did everything and nothing happened but what is His will. Although this doctrine that God is responsible and controls everything is so prevalent in the church today, this scripture is saying just the opposite. You need to fear—be cautious, aware, and diligent—lest you miss out on something that God has provided for you.

Harden Not Your Heart

For unto us was the gospel preached, as well as unto them: but the word preached did not profit them, not being mixed with faith in them that heard it.

Hebrews 4:2

This verse perfectly states what we've been talking about. God, by grace, had provided a plan. He promised Abraham in Genesis 15 that He would bring his descendants out of the land of Egypt and give them the entire nation of Canaan and all the surrounding nations too. (Gen. 15:18–21.) God made this promise four hundred and thirty years before it came to pass. When He finally led the people out, they didn't put faith in His purpose and plan so that generation never saw it come to pass. They died in the wilderness. They came out of the land of Egypt, but they died in the wilderness because of their unbelief.

You have to mix faith with what God wants you to do. You must listen and obey Him. You have to believe God in order to see His promises come to pass in your life.

The Sabbath Rest

For we which have believed do enter into rest, as he said, As I have sworn in my wrath...

Hebrews 4:3

The writer of Hebrews now begins to quote from Psalm 95, which he also quoted back in Hebrews 3.

While it is said, To day if ye will hear his voice, harden not your hearts, as in the provocation.

Hebrews 3:15

Here is the passage from Psalm 95 being referred to:

To day if ye will hear his voice, Harden not your heart, as in the provocation, and as in the day of temptation in the wilderness: When your fathers tempted me, proved me, and saw my work. Forty years long was I grieved with this generation, and said, It is a people that do err in their heart, and they have not known my ways: Unto whom I sware in my wrath that they should not enter into my rest.

Psalm 95:7–11

In both Hebrews 3 and 4, the writer is making reference back to this scripture that David wrote under the inspiration of the Holy Spirit. Fully, Hebrews 4:3 says:

For we which have believed do enter into rest, as he said, As I have sworn in my wrath, if they shall enter into my rest: although the works were finished from the foundation of the world.

The reference at the end of this verse links the rest that Psalm 95 spoke of to the Sabbath rest that God took in Genesis 2:2. After He created the heavens and the earth, God rested from all of His works.

*For he spake in a certain place of the seventh day on this wise,
And God did rest the seventh day from all his works.*

Hebrews 4:4

This reference in Hebrews 4:4 is taken from Genesis 2:2. Hebrews 4 goes on to say:

*Seeing therefore it remaineth that some must enter therein, and
they to whom it was first preached entered not in because of unbelief: Again, he limiteth a certain day, saying in David, To day, after
so long a time; as it is said, To day if ye will hear his voice, harden
not your hearts.*

Hebrews 4:6–7

In a nutshell, these words are Old English for "Don't be like the Jews who missed out on something that God provided." The writer of Hebrews quotes this scripture of David to remind us that there remains a rest to the people of God, a rest first spoken of in Genesis 2 when it says God rested on the seventh day from all of His labors. It goes on to say that this rest, this special relationship, obviously wasn't fulfilled when the Jews occupied the land of Canaan because David came along over four hundred years later in Psalm 95 still saying that there remains a rest for the people of God.

Type and Shadow

The point of this passage is to let us know that this spiritual rest wasn't fulfilled when the Jews occupied the Promised Land because over four centuries later, David said that there is still a rest for the people of God.

> *For if Jesus* [Greek translation of Hebrew name Joshua] *had given them rest, then would he not afterward have spoken of another day.*
>
> Hebrews 4:8

This word "Jesus" is just the Greek word for *Joshua*. Joshua and Jesus are the same word in different languages. In context, this isn't talking about our Lord Jesus Christ. This is saying that if Joshua, the one who led the children of Israel into the Promised Land, would have fulfilled this promise about there being a rest to the people of God, then David, hundreds of years later, wouldn't have spoken about this rest yet to be fulfilled.

This passage reveals that the rest these verses were promising was not fulfilled when the Jews occupied the land of Canaan. It's saying that there is a rest reserved for the people of God, and that applies to us today as New Testament believers.

> *For if Jesus* [Joshua] *had given them rest, then would he* [David] *not afterward have spoken of another day. There remaineth therefore a rest to the people of God. For he that is entered into his rest, he also hath ceased from his own works, as God did from his.*
>
> Hebrews 4:8–10

Keep in mind, this refers back to the creation when God rested on the seventh day. The rest of God—the Sabbath day—was a picture, a type and shadow of what was to come.

Chapter 14

God Anticipated

There are only two places in all of scripture where a reason for the Sabbath was given. In the Old Testament, Exodus 20:8–11 says that the Sabbath is for you, your family, your servants, and your animals to rest. The second time the Sabbath is mentioned and the reason for it explained is in Colossians.

> *Let no man therefore judge you in meat, or in drink, or in respect of an holyday, or of the new moon, or of the sabbath days: Which are a shadow of things to come; but the body is of Christ.*
>
> Colossians 2:16–17

Verse 17 reveals that all five of these things listed in verse 16, including the Sabbath, were a shadow of something that was to come. In the Old Testament, they didn't have the reality of Christ. All of the blood sacrifices and rituals were symbolic of something yet to come. Types, shadows, pictures, and symbols are very important if you don't have the real thing in front of you.

For instance, imagine that you had never seen me before. If somebody drew a picture of me and showed it to you, it could give you an idea of what I look like. But why would you keep looking at my picture if I were standing right there in front of you? A picture is useful only if the person isn't there.

If I were standing just around the corner of a building from you, you couldn't see me, but you could see my shadow. My shadow could give you a lot of information about me. Although you couldn't see me, from my shadow you could tell whether I'm standing still, moving towards or away from you, or jumping up and down. You could get an idea about whether I was fat or skinny, tall or short. But if I walked around the corner of the building and came into full view, what would you think of the person who fell to the ground trying to hug and shake hands with my shadow? If you can't see me, my shadow might be the next best thing, but if I'm right there in plain view, why would you keep looking at my shadow?

A New Testament Reality

In Colossians 2:16–17, the Bible says that these five things—one of which was the Sabbath—were a shadow of things to come but not the very image of those things. They were just a shadow. Yet, we have Christians today who are trying to observe the Sabbath. There are entire denominations built around observing the Sabbath. Sabbath observance is rigidly enforced. They preach that you're a Sabbath-breaker if you work on the Sabbath. They have missed the whole symbolism of the Sabbath.

God Anticipated

The Sabbath isn't picturing a day. The Sabbath was observed in the Old Testament, but now it's a New Testament reality. That's what Hebrews 4 is talking about. The Sabbath was a picture of a rest—a relationship with God where you are trusting and relying on the finished work of Christ and not your own effort and performance. To prove this, the writer of Hebrews 4 begins to talk about the Sabbath that the Lord instituted way back in Genesis 2.

> On the seventh day God ended his work which he had made; and he rested on the seventh day from all his work which he had made. And God blessed the seventh day.
>
> Genesis 2:2–3

When the Lord created the heavens and the earth, there was an order to the way He created things. He didn't create man on the first day of creation. Man was the crown jewel of all God's creation. Why didn't He create man first? Because things weren't ready for him! If God would have created man on the first day of creation, man would have had to tread water for four days before there was any land to stand on. Had he created man after the land was created but before the trees had been spoken into existence, man would have had to dodge all of these full-grown trees popping up everywhere. Contrary to what evolution says, the trees didn't come from plants and grow gradually. It didn't take millions and billions of years. For more information on this topic, please check out my message entitled, *Evolution*. Although God was busy creating these things the first few days, the earth still wasn't ready for man.

Abundantly Provided

The Lord waited until the entire creation was done before He made man. The fruit trees were created full grown. They already had fruit on them. Man didn't have to wait seven years for those trees to start producing fruit. God created a perfect world for man. There was land to stand on, food to eat, air to breathe, and the temperature was just right. God made animals for man's pleasure. He made everything perfect.

> *God called the light Day, and the darkness he called Night. And the evening and the morning were the first day...And the evening and the morning were the second day.*
>
> Genesis 1:5,8

The Hebrews count time from sundown one day until sundown the next day. They don't count time from twelve o'clock midnight until the next twelve o'clock midnight. They count it evening to evening.

On the first day, the Lord started at sundown and went through to the next day. Then right before sundown at the end of the sixth day, He created man. God created man at the very end of all of His creation. He had already created all of the food. Everything was perfect for man. Then, immediately, God rested and entered into the seventh day. So man was created right before this Sabbath, and man entered into God's Sabbath where everything was already abundantly provided.

God had anticipated every need, not only of Adam and Eve, but also for the entire human race. God has created everything we need. If

126

there were ten times as many people on this planet, God has made the earth to be able to sustain us. He's anticipated everything.

God Rested

God isn't creating things today. He isn't making new plants, new animals, or new people.

God said, Let the earth bring forth grass, the herb yielding seed, and the fruit tree yielding fruit after his kind, whose seed is in itself, upon the earth: and it was so.

Genesis 1:11

God didn't just say, "Let there be trees. Let there be fruit." If He had only said that and didn't create a way for them to reproduce, then the Lord would have to create new trees every time an old one died to maintain the balance. He would have to say, "Let there be a million new cows today," and He'd have to create new cows. But when He created the animals, He said:

Be fruitful, and multiply.

Genesis 1:22

God gave plants, animals, people—everything—the ability to reproduce. When God finished the creation saying, "Behold, it is good," and then rested, it wasn't just symbolic. God, literally, has not created anything since the original creation. His original creation is self-perpetuating.

God created it this way so that when He rested, He literally quit. It's over. This doesn't mean that He rested in the sense that He was tired. It wasn't as if one more moon and God was going to pass out from sheer exhaustion. It's not that He didn't have it in Him to create just one more cow, horse, or tree. No, that's not that kind of rest God is taking. It's like an artist who has painted a beautiful picture. Everything is perfect. Adding just one more brush stroke would ruin it. So they put their paintbrush down and rest from their work, not because they're worn out from holding the brush up, but because their masterpiece is complete. It's done. It's finished. Lawyers say, "I rest my case." That doesn't mean they're worn out or that they can't say one more word. It just means that they're finished. They're through. In this way, God rested.

The Lord doesn't get tired like man does. (Isa. 40:28.) God rested because everything was so perfect. When man came and said, "Lord, I'm hungry," God didn't have to say, "Oh, I didn't think of that. Here, let Me create a fruit tree for you to eat something." No, He had anticipated every need, and He rested. Man didn't have to ask God for something. All man had to do was reach out and take what God had already created and say, "Thank You." This is what the rest, and the Old Testament Sabbath picture, was all about.

"Trust Me for Everything"

God told His people to take one day a week off while everybody else was working their fingers to the bone. In the natural realm, that doesn't make sense. *How can I prosper as much as other people who work seven days a week if I only work six?* If it's just you and your effort, you can't. But if it's God blessing the work of your hands, you can. If God is your Source and you're trusting and obeying Him, then taking one day off out of every seven will actually make you prosper more than those people who only rely on their own ability. Since there was faith involved, the Jews prospered more than the other nations around them even though they took one day in seven off.

According to Leviticus 25, God told His people to take one year in seven off as well. He promised to bless them, just like clockwork, with three times the normal harvest in that sixth year because they were resting and trusting in Him. That supernatural triple harvest in the sixth year took them through the end of the sixth year, the seventh year when they rested, and the eighth year when they planted their new crops and waited on the harvest. This is what the Sabbath was portraying. The Sabbath never was about observing a certain day. The Lord hates this attitude of people who only serve Him one day a week. Through the Sabbath picture, God wanted to communicate to His people this truth, "I'm your Source. Trust Me for everything."

Today, many folks are enforcing a Sabbath day. I was raised in a semi-legalistic home. It wasn't as bad as some, but we didn't mow the grass, wash the dishes, or do any other housework on Sunday. To us, that was the Sabbath.

I know now that Sunday isn't the Sabbath. Some people who have become aware of this simply changed the day to Saturday (e.g., Seventh-Day Adventists), yet, they continued missing the point. The reason the Church started meeting on Sunday was because it was the day that Jesus was raised from the dead. They had a revelation that we are redeemed from the Old Testament types and shadows. Now that we're living in the reality of trusting Jesus, they made a clean break between the Old Testament law and the New Testament.

Yet many New Testament Christians today still have a Sabbath-keeping mentality. They feel guilty if they go out and do certain things on the Sabbath. Some people keep the Sabbath on Saturday. Others are mean about enforcing whatever Sabbath day they observe. Even I fell prey to this thinking as I used to drive forty minutes out of the way so I wouldn't have to go through a tollbooth and pay someone to work on Sunday.

"I Depend on You"

In the very beginning of my ministry, I held a revival meeting on a Sunday morning. A group from the church wanted to take me out to eat, but I told them, "No way! I'm not going to go out to eat and help somebody work on the Sabbath. I refuse to help them be a Sabbath-breaker." The big group of people who were there to take me out ended up going to eat by themselves because I didn't go.

You might be thinking, *That's a little legalistic.* Well, if you're going to believe it, believe it. If you want to go back and observe the Old Testament Sabbath, then it would be more appropriate to do like the Pharisees did. They dictated the number of steps that you could walk on a Sabbath Day.

John the Baptist was probably raised by the Essenes, the same people who wrote the Dead Sea Scrolls. Their writings reveal that it was considered work to have a bowel movement on the Sabbath Day. Therefore, this was against the law in their eyes. If you're going to believe it, believe it. It's hypocritical to be partially under the law and observe just a little bit of it. Either we're under the Sabbath, or we aren't.

In actuality, the Sabbath was only a picture of trusting God to where you cease from your own labors saying, "God, I believe that You're my Source. I'm not going to depend on just my efforts alone. I'm going to depend on You." This is what it pictured.

Enter His Rest

God created everything, and rested. He doesn't have to create food for you to eat or air for you to breathe. He created the earth in such a way that the trees clean the air so there's a perpetual supply of oxygen. God doesn't have to create anything for us. He already anticipated all of our needs, and He's already made everything. Now we have entered into His rest. We are benefiting from all of the things that God created when He anticipated the needs of the entire human race.

This is one reason I strongly disagree with the people who say that we're destroying the earth. Really, it's a slap in God's face to think that man could overwhelm, overtax, and destroy this earth He's created. Take, for instance, Mount St. Helens. Scientists said it would take ten thousand years for this mountain to regenerate. Within three years, Mount St. Helens has done what they thought it would take ten thousand years to do. The earth has the ability to regenerate and cleanse itself. A polluted stream will purify itself in a short period of time if you just stop polluting it. This secular, ungodly attitude has exalted man to the position of god, and God has been eliminated or significantly decreased. They don't realize that God anticipated everything we could ever do.

This earth isn't going to be destroyed by us. God will destroy it with a fervent heat. We aren't going to destroy ourselves.

God anticipated everything. He made all things, and we've just entered into His rest. We are benefiting from what God created thousands of years ago. It's already complete. All we're doing is reaching out and appropriating what God has already provided. That's what the Sabbath was a picture of.

Chapter 15
Labor to Rest

In this New Testament age, we now have the reality that the Sabbath only pictured. We are resting and trusting in what God has done through the Lord Jesus Christ. We now have a relationship with God, and He's already provided everything we'll ever need.

Before you ever needed healing, God had already healed you.

> *By whose stripes ye were healed.*
>
> 1 Peter 2:24

You don't have to ask God to heal you. You don't have to do something, and then, in response to your action, God heals you. No, healing is already provided. All you have to do is just reach out, take it, and say, "Thank You."

You don't have to ask God to bless you. The Lord has commanded the blessing upon you in everything that you do. Before you were ever born, before you ever had a need, the blessing of God was already on you. You don't have to beg God for supply. Just rest in

Him and trust, saying, "Father, I know You've already met my needs." This rest is what the Sabbath portrayed. This is the rest spoken of in Hebrews 4.

Very few Christians today are resting in what Jesus has already provided. Instead, they're operating with the mind-set that they have a problem and they need God to do something. They're waiting on God to create, to move, to do something new to meet their need. They don't understand that God anticipated their need. They aren't resting in the Lord, as Hebrews 4 describes.

"Father, It's Done"

After saying all these things, the writer of Hebrews said:

> For he that is entered into his rest, he also hath ceased from his own works, as God did from his.
>
> Hebrews 4:10

In other words, for people who have entered into this rest, they have ceased trying to make God do something. They've ceased trying to get God to bless them. They've ceased trying to earn His favor. And now they are just resting in the truth that, through Jesus, God has already supplied everything. In the same way that God created everything and now He doesn't have to create new plants, animals, or people today because they simply propagate as a result of His original creation, the Lord made a new creation—and that's us.

Therefore if any man be in Christ, he is a new creature: old things are passed away; behold, all things are become new.

2 Corinthians 5:17

We are a new creation in our born-again spirit and in this new creation, when we need to be healed, God doesn't have to heal us. Healing is already in the spirit part of us—that new creation. When we need to be prospered, God doesn't have to prosper us. He has already commanded blessing and prosperity into our spirit man. He has blessed us with all spiritual blessings in heavenly places. Now, in the new creation through Jesus, everything is already done.

The key to the Christian life is learning how to rest. Trust that the Father says it's done. My bankbook may say I'm broke, and I'm on the verge of bawling and squalling. I may have a strong desire to start praying, fasting, and doing something to make God move. But I'm going to rest and trust His Word. His Word says that He has already supplied all my needs. He's already blessed me. He's commanded His blessing upon me. I am blessed above all people. The Christian life is learning how to rest, not how to work and do something to make God move. That's what this passage is talking about.

Trusting and Relying

If you have entered into His rest, then you have ceased from your own efforts. It's no longer you doing something to make God move. It's you learning how to trust and rely on the truth that God has already done it.

Let us labour therefore to enter into that rest, lest any man fall after the same example of unbelief.

Hebrews 4:11

This sounds like an oxymoron—a contradiction of terms. How do you labor to rest? This isn't saying that we should just "veg out," go to sleep, and do nothing. This is ceasing from your own works, from thinking that you have to earn God's favor. It's ceasing from thinking you have to do something to motivate God to get Him to love you and answer your prayers.

Saying, "Oh God, don't You love this person? I've been praying for them for twenty years. Oh, God, do something!" isn't resting. You think you're the one motivating God and if it wasn't for your intercession, the Lord would just let people go to hell because He doesn't care. If you think it's your great intercession that is moving God, you're trusting in your own effort. You aren't resting in Him.

Rest is simply trusting and relying on God. It's saying, "Lord, You love this person more than I ever could. You've already provided salvation for them, so I know it's Your will that they be saved. Father, I thank You that Your will is coming to pass. Here am I. Use me. If You can open up a door for me to share Your love and Your Word with this person, then I will do it." That's how you pray for lost people. Don't plead with God as if it's up to Him whether or not they get saved. He's not the one determining who gets saved. God has made the provision. He's provided salvation for everybody, but each person has to decide to accept that salvation. So you can only become a channel for God to flow through.

Depend on God

When you understand rest properly, you understand it takes effort to rest. You must labor to rest. When the banker is calling, your checkbook is in the red, and your spouse has been saying, "You've got to do something!" it takes labor to say, "My faith is in God. I'm doing what He has told me to do. I trust Him and I'm not going to panic. I refuse to get out of rest. I'm not going to get into fear." When the doctor says you're going to die, it takes labor for you to respond, "That's not what God's Word says. By His stripes I was healed! I'm not going to be healed, I was already healed. He's already supplied healing, and I'm not going to panic. I refuse to get into fear." It takes effort for you to rest like that.

This is why we study the Word. We don't study the Word to get God to heal us. We study the Word to find out that God has already healed us, to calm our fears, and to anchor our faith. Then we can say, "Father, I'm operating on this knowledge that You've given me, and I'm not moving off of it!" This takes effort.

In the area of finances, I'm still learning to rest and growing. I haven't mastered this area by any means; however, I'm seeing God's supply in a way that I've never before seen in my life. In 2009, Andrew Wommack Ministries must have over $20 million a year just to break even, as we give many of our materials away at no charge. If you were to think about this and take the responsibility upon yourself for producing this money, you'd lose sleep. We must have around $2,000 per hour, twenty-four hours a day, 365 days per year to cover our expenses. Raising such a sum is just beyond my ability, and I know it so I have to labor to rest. I have to keep my attention focused on God, saying, "Lord, this is what You called me to do. You're the One who told me to do this. Therefore, it's Your responsibility to finance this ministry, not mine." Strangely, the bigger the financial needs of the ministry get, the easier it is for me to rest. You might think it's the opposite, but it's not.

Back when we were small, I remember going through a really bad time financially. I had a dream one night. In this dream, I just quit the ministry and joined the Air Force. I was going to pay off all of the debts I had incurred in ministry. It would take years, but I could—eventually—pay it off. Since I'm what they call a "lucid dreamer," I dream in color. My dreams seem so vivid and real to me that sometimes it's hard for me to tell whether I'm dreaming or not. That night, I woke up with a start. I laid there in bed thinking, *Oh, it was just a dream. Thank You, Jesus, that I didn't join the Air Force.* Then Jamie leaned over and said, "It wasn't so bad that you had to go join the Air Force." My heart started pounding as I thought, *Oh, God. It wasn't a dream!* I found out later that I had been talking in my sleep and she had heard the whole thing.

Back when our ministry was small and we had $20,000 indebtedness, I could pay that off in my own strength if I had to. But at the level we now operate on, I can't pay off millions and millions of dollars of indebtedness. So actually, it's easier for me to rest now because I'm in way over my head. I know that if God doesn't come through, I've had it, so it's been years since I've worried about finances. Now that my needs are way beyond my ability to provide, I have to depend on God.

"Do Something!"

Our flesh wants to get into "do something" mode. You feel the need to start praying, fasting, or doing something else to try to make God come through. Every time you do that, you've stepped out of faith in what God has already done and you've moved into legalism and works. You're going to do something to make yourself worthy. You're going to do something so that God has to come through. The moment you've done that, you're out of grace and faith and into legalism. Your sin isn't as truly offensive to God as your self-righteousness and self-dependence. It's as if Jesus isn't enough; you're going to do something and go through your own strength instead of through Jesus. That's the most offensive thing you could possibly do.

In a sense, you're saying, "Jesus isn't enough. I have to do something to motivate God. He has to move in my life because of what I've done." God has already provided everything. The Sabbath illustrated this. The same way He created everything for man and all man had to do was just reach out and receive, so it is now in the new creation. God has provided everything for you. It's just a matter of reaching out and appropriating by faith what God has already provided by grace.

This is going to take some effort. You'll have to study the Word. This is not to so impress God with your Bible study that He will move because you're so holy. You need to study the Word to renew your mind. You aren't going to hear very many other people say what I'm saying. You aren't going to get this teaching watching *As the Stomach Turns* on the television. You're going to have to get into the Word of God and receive sound Bible teaching. You'll have to turn off the television and start studying the Word. You're going to have to spend time in the presence of God. It's going to take effort. You'll have to labor to rest.

When the pressure is on and the devil is screaming, "Do something. Do something!" trying to get you to take matters into your own hands, the hardest thing you'll ever do is stand there and say, "My faith is in God, and if He doesn't come through, I'm dead." That's it. It takes effort to rest. It takes a lot of faith to rest.

God has already provided everything. You just need to rest in it.

It Takes Effort

There have been times when I've rested by praising God for what His Word says He's done, not what I see or feel. When I first begin to praise, I don't feel like praising God. I feel like crying and running because I don't feel like God is working. But when I take a step of faith and continue praising Him, saying, "Father, I thank You that I am healed. I thank You that I am blessed. I thank You that I am what Your Word says I am," then I begin resting in Him.

I may start in the flesh. I may not really feel like praising, but I'll do it because I know it's the right thing to do. And if I'll keep at it, I'll start listening to myself and truly believing that I am healed. I do believe that God has supplied my needs. I do believe that He has already done this. After a while, true faith begins to rise up in my heart. Then, I'm not praising anymore just because I know it's the right thing to do. I praise because I really believe in God's provision.

The moment I get over into faith—where faith is mixed with God's grace—boom! The power of God is released and I see the things of God come to pass.

This is going to take effort. You can't just float through your circumstances with the crowd. You'll have to swim against the current. You're going to have to go against your feelings and against what the circumstances say. It takes effort.

These truths are working in my life and they'll work for you, too. God has already anticipated everything. Everything that you need is already done. You don't need to badger God, asking and pleading with Him. He has anticipated every need you could ever have. God has already made provision for you. It's there. Now you just have to rest. You have to get into a position where you believe—not just say you believe. Faith is an active force on the inside of you, but it takes effort to release it. First, you must know and understand this truth that God has already supplied for your needs.

Chapter 16
Understanding God's Love

In the new creation, through what Jesus did, God has already provided everything we need. We just need to learn what has been provided by grace. Then we must learn how to rest in it, trusting God and appropriating what He's already provided by faith.

Although this foundational truth has many applications, the number one way it has affected me is in my personal relationship with God. It has deeply affected my understanding of how much God loves me. Everything else in the Christian life comes as a result of relationship.

So many people are trying to work some kind of a formula. They're looking for some kind of a key, for two or three steps they can follow, something they can do. They treat God like He's a slot machine. "Give me something I can stick in there and pull the handle so that I can make God come out." It doesn't work that way.

The most important truth I've learned from all this is that God's love for me is unconditional. It's not based on anything I do. God's love toward me is consistent. It never fluctuates based on my performance. When I'm better, God doesn't love me more. When I'm bad, God doesn't love me less. I have come to recognize that God's grace—and therefore, God's love, favor, and acceptance of me—is unconditional. It has nothing to do with who I am. It has everything to do with who He is. It's not because I am lovely, it's because He is love. This is one of the greatest applications of this truth.

Uncontrolled Feelings

In this was manifested the love of God toward us, because that God sent his only begotten Son into the world, that we might live through him.

1 John 4:9

How do we know that God loves us? Such knowledge is not based on a feeling, or emotion. Feelings and emotions can be dangerous. Ephesians 4:19 says of the godless that they, going beyond, or...

...past feeling have given themselves over unto lasciviousness...

Since *lasciviousness* isn't a word that we use often today, many people just skip over it without really thinking about what it means. *Lasciviousness* is uncontrolled, unrestrained, unfettered lust and desire. This scripture is describing a coming generation of people who have given themselves over to lasciviousness—uncontrolled, unrestrained emotions, feelings, and desires that go beyond a natural, normal use of feelings. I believe we live in that generation.

This generation today has gone far beyond what God ever intended our emotions to be. People today have elevated emotions to a level that is absolutely ungodly.

I've talked to thousands of people who have told me that they're depressed. I've asked them, "What's the problem? What is it that's depressing you?" They answer, "Well, nothing specific I can think of, but I just feel this." They don't have a reason for their depression other than, "I feel this."

We've elevated feelings to the point where if we don't feel something, then it must not be true. Feelings are fickle. God gave them to us, and in their proper place they're okay. But when you let your feelings dominate you, you're acting like a child. Children say, "Well, I don't feel like doing it." As the parent, you have to say, "I don't care if you feel like doing it or not. I told you to do it. Now get up and do it." You don't always feel like going to work, but part of being an adult is you get up and do what you need to do. Only a spoiled, affluent generation like what we live in has the luxury of doing what they feel like.

"Hard Keepers"

One or two generations ago, people were struggling to survive. It didn't matter how they felt. They didn't have time to sit around and discern their feelings. They were too busy scratching out a living and doing what it took to make ends meet. But now we sit around thinking, *I don't feel like you love me anymore. I don't feel like doing this.* You can't praise God when your thumb is in the way. Pull it out of your mouth, grow up, and quit letting feelings dominate you!

People have come to me by the thousands saying, "But I don't feel God loves me."

I answer, "Well then, your feelings are wrong."

"Oh, but I've got to feel it."

"Why do you have to feel it?"

"It's not real if I don't feel it."

That's stupid! And it's this same attitude that is destroying a lot of marriages today. It would be wonderful if every spouse treated their mate exactly the way they were supposed to, but you're married to a fallen human being. They don't always say or do things just right. You need to grow up and give your spouse a little bit of slack sometimes. It doesn't matter that they don't always treat you perfectly, do what's right—not what you feel like.

You may not feel like they love you, but you know that they do. Perhaps your spouse doesn't tell you enough that they love you. Some people are just what I call "hard keepers."

You can nearly starve some horses and they'll still look full. These are "easy keepers." Other horses you can feed and feed and feed until they die of colic because they've eaten so much, yet they still look poor. These are called "hard keepers." We've become hard keepers today because we have elevated feelings to a place where we must "feel" to believe. That's immature and childish. There is a place for emotions, but not the prominent place it occupies with most people.

We have gone beyond feelings into lasciviousness—to where we have to feel everything.

Rule Your Emotions

Some people may know what the truth is, but it doesn't matter. They are ruled by whatever they feel. That's very carnal. It's demonic. It's a perversion of the way that God made us to be.

A while back I listened to a tape of someone ministering. Most of what this minister said was really good; however in one of her examples, she was talking about a friend's daughter who had a certain problem. She was counseling the girl and trying to deal with her when the daughter said, "But my parents didn't treat me right. They didn't honor me. They didn't do this and they didn't do that." This lady on the tape said, "I knew the parents. These were good parents. They weren't perfect. They didn't do everything right. But what the daughter was saying about them wasn't true. Although they weren't perfect, these parents loved and honored that daughter."

Then this minister said, "I knew this girl was wrong, but I didn't correct her because it didn't matter whether she was right or wrong. To her it was real." When this minister said that, I immediately popped the tape out and threw it away. This is false teaching and I hate that. I hate it with a passion.

Some people may say, "But that's right. To the individual, those feelings are real." Such teaching is deceptive. It's the truth that's going to set you free. (John 8:32.) The proper thing to do would have been to stop this girl in the middle of that and say, "Your perception is wrong, and until you start wising up and realizing that not everybody is going to stroke you and treat you perfectly the rest of your life, and until you quit blaming other people for the offense that you've taken, and until you start shouldering your own responsibility, you're never going to grow and mature."

You may feel some things so passionately that it doesn't matter to you whether it's truth or not. It's true to you. I'm telling you, it's only the truth—the real truth, not the "truth" that you feel—that's going to set you free. If this is an issue you struggle with, I recommend my teaching entitled, *Harnessing Your Emotions*. God intends for you to rule your emotions, not for your emotions to rule you.

"I Just Don't Feel It"

When people come up to me saying, "Would you please pray for me? I just don't feel the love of God." I'll begin to speak to them 1 John 4:9, saying, "Don't you know that God loves you? Jesus came and died for you."

"Oh, I know that Jesus died for me. And I know that God loves me. But I just don't feel it."

When I hear that, the spirit of slap just comes all over me. You know that God loves you, but you don't feel it. You don't have a goose bump. You don't have a feeling overwhelming you at the moment. And so, because you don't feel loved, forget the truth. Forget reality. Forget the Word. You just don't feel it.

To pray that we would "have a feeling" is lasciviousness. It's inordinate, perverse, and demonic! You don't have to always feel something.

No Excuse

In this was manifested the love of God toward us, because that God sent his only begotten Son into the world, that we might live through him.

1 John 4:9

For God so loved the world, that he gave his only begotten Son, that whosoever believeth in him should not perish, but have everlasting life.

John 3:16

If you comprehend these scriptures, you have zero excuse for ever being depressed, discouraged, defeated, or feeling lonely. You might think you have reasons, but you have no excuse. You have the knowledge it takes to set you free from the rule of emotion if you would just meditate on the truth saying, "Father, You love me."

But God commendeth his love toward us, in that, while we were yet sinners, Christ died for us.

Romans 5:8

This love that God gave us through Jesus didn't come in response to your goodness, or because you've merited it by praying, fasting, and studying the Word. It wasn't because you humbled yourself and started being a good person. Think about what this verse says: God commended His love toward us—even died for us—while we were yet sinners!

A Religious Hypocrite

You may have been a "good" sinner or a "bad" one, but we've all sinned and come short of His glory. (Rom. 3:23.) Compared to other people, you might look good, but compared to Jesus, we are all an offense against God. We have all fallen short of where God wanted us to be. The Lord doesn't look down on anyone and say, "Oh, they're so close. They are so good that I've got to help them and give them a little bit of a boost." No, from God's perspective—perfection—we've all fallen short of what He wants us to be. None of us was worth God sending His Son to die in our place. No one deserves the love of God.

Before you can really understand how much God loves you, you have to quit loving yourself so much. You must quit thinking that you are such a feather in God's cap that He just couldn't live without you. You must come to the end of yourself, quit trusting in yourself, and recognize where you are.

Although I had already been born again at age eight, the experience that turned my life around came when I was eighteen years old. I had become a religious Pharisee. I was living such a holy life that I was holier than the pastor of our church! I was leading more people to the Lord per week than he was. I've never in all of my life spoken a word of profanity. I'm almost sixty years old now. I've never taken a drink of liquor, smoked a cigarette, or even tasted coffee.

I was living a holy life, but I had fallen into this deception of trusting in my own goodness. As long as I thought that God owed something to me, I would never have a great revelation of how much He loved me. But on March 23, 1968, when I was eighteen years old, God just pulled back a curtain from before my eyes. It was a supernatural revelation. He shined His light on me and I saw myself for who I really was. Although I had been born again, I was a religious hypocrite.

The Beginning of God

You may have lied, stolen, committed sexual immorality, and done all kinds of other things that I never did, but I doubt very seriously that you have ever seen yourself as more of a sinner than I have. I saw myself from God's perspective. I saw how vile I was—my hypocrisy, my religiosity—and I came to the end of myself. I turned myself inside out confessing my sin for over an hour. I fully expected the Lord to kill me. I had been told that God was the One who killed my dad when I was twelve years old. I thought that God judged us. When I saw how bad I was, I thought it was the first time God had seen it too, and I fully expected Him to kill me on the spot. Honestly, I'm not exaggerating. I never expected to live through the night. So I just confessed everything—not only my actions, but my thoughts, emotions, and attitudes too. I turned myself inside out, hoping that before God killed me, I would repent enough that He would at least take me into heaven.

To my surprise, when I humbled myself and quit putting any faith or confidence in myself, the love of God flowed into my life in a way that just revolutionized me. For four and a half months, I was caught up in the presence of God. The Lord just loved me. Yet I never would have understood the depth of God's love if I were thinking there was something I did to deserve it.

If you are still maintaining your own righteousness, then you'll never truly understand God's love. You have to come to the end of yourself. That's why God gave the Old Testament Law, to expose how ungodly we were—to bring us to the end of ourselves. The law condemns. It's harsh. Its purpose was to bring you to the end of yourself because only when you come to the end of yourself do you find the beginning of God.

Chapter 17

Unconditional

❦

God, by grace, commended His love towards us. While we were yet sinners, Christ died for us. He didn't see something in you that was just so wonderful He had to have you. .

> But God, who is rich in mercy, for his great love wherewith he loved us.
>
> Ephesians 2:4

The Lord was motivated to love us not because we are lovely, but because He is love. This is what the balance of grace and faith has taught me. God's love for me is not tied to any worth or value of my own.

Self-Esteem vs. Christ-Esteem

You may think that this teaching is depressing or discouraging. You may wonder what I'm trying to do to your sense of self-worth. Your self is what made it necessary for Jesus to come to this earth and die. Your self may be better than my self, but it still has caused a lot of heartache and pain in both your life and the lives of others too.

As a believer in Jesus, I am not into self-esteem—I'm into Christ-esteem. I esteem what Jesus has done. I am thrilled with who I am in Christ, what God has done in me, but there is a part of me that is corrupt. There's a part that I deny and reject as I walk in the Spirit. (Gal. 5:16.) There's a part of me that's still not born again. My spirit is born again, but I still have flesh so there's a part of me that I don't esteem.

There are times when you feel absolutely rotten. There are times when you act like the devil. When you act stupid, you ought to feel stupid. God gave us emotions just as He gave us feeling in our hands. If you weren't paying attention and leaned up against a hot stove, you could do irreparable damage to yourself. But God gave you the ability to feel pain. None of us like to feel pain, but if you put your hand on a hot stove, the pain you feel in your hand will remind you to withdraw it before you seriously injure yourself.

God gave you the ability to feel depressed and discouraged, but not so you could live there.

All About God

The Bible says in Isaiah 26:3, the Lord will...

> ...keep him in perfect peace, whose mind is stayed on thee: because he trusteth in thee.

If you're depressed, you aren't keeping your mind stayed on God. You're looking at circumstances. You've let your attention move off of Jesus, the Author and Finisher of your faith. (Heb. 12:2.) The reason you're sinking into depression is because you quit looking at Jesus. You started looking at the wind and the waves around you, which caused you to fear. (Matt. 14:30.) There's a purpose for your feelings.

When discouragement comes against me, I don't ignore it. I recognize that it's there because I haven't been meditating on God. I haven't been focused on the Lord the way that I should. Once I get back to focusing on the Lord, my feelings realign to the Word.

When I'm not feeling right, I don't stop believing that God loves me because I don't feel His love. I have written this truth in my heart. It's an absolute—a cardinal rule that I never deviate from.

But God commendeth his love toward us, in that, while we were yet sinners, Christ died for us.

Romans 5:8

That means God's love has nothing to do with my goodness or anything in me. It's all about God.

Much More Now

Much more then, being now justified by his blood, we shall be saved from wrath through him.

Romans 5:9

God loved you by His grace—not based on your performance. If He loved you while you were yet a sinner so much that He died for you, then how much more does He love you now that you're born again!

The average church teaches a watered-down version of God's love now. They won't admit to it, but their attitude shows it. They say, "Come to the Lord just as you are. If you're a sinner, that means you're qualified. Jesus died for sinners." But what would happen if someone came into a church service drunk and reeking of alcohol? The typical Christian would walk up and say, "God loves you. He has a better life for you. Jesus died for your sins. Wouldn't You like to receive Him? Wouldn't you like to be forgiven?" The average Christian will extend grace towards a lost man, but what happens when that drunk prays to receive salvation and then comes back again drunk the next week? Once this person claims to be a believer, the average Christian would turn on him, telling him, "God is mad at you. He isn't going to bless you. God won't answer your prayers. The wrath of God is coming on you. You'd better repent, or else! Turn or burn!" They'd start preaching wrath to him.

This is the reason a lot of people go through what's called a "honeymoon" period when they get born again. As a sinner, they're told, "Regardless of what you've done, God loves you by grace. It's unconditional. It doesn't matter what you've done. Come, accept Jesus, and you'll get all of your sins forgiven." The person says, "That's good news," and they believe. They receive salvation and are just so in love with God. Colors are brighter, sounds are better, and smells are nicer. Everything is wonderful because they believe that God loves them.

"What's Wrong?"

Then that new Christian goes to church. He hears somebody testify that they were healed of something and they think, *Well, I have something. I'd like to be healed too.* The Church prays for them, but they don't instantly see a manifestation of their healing. So they begin to ask, "What's wrong?" The Church answers, "Sin." Confused, the new Christian says, "I thought God had forgiven me."

And here is the answer they get from these well-meaning church people: "Oh, yeah. He had back then. But you've sinned since then. You're going to have to start studying more. You're going to have to read the Bible an hour a day, pray in tongues, and go to church. Have you been paying your tithes? God won't bless you unless you pay your tithes."

All of a sudden, the feeling they once had that God loves them unconditionally based on grace is replaced with, *Uh-oh! If I'm going to receive from God, I need to start being holy. I need to do all of these things or God won't bless me.* They stop putting faith in grace, and they're now trying to merit and earn God's favor instead.

Romans 5:8 reveals that God loved you so much that while you were yet a sinner Christ died for you. Romans 5:9 says that much more now are you saved from wrath through Him. You may have come to Christ while you were living in adultery. You confessed Jesus as your Lord, believing in your heart that He was raised from the dead, and instantly you were in relationship with God. Adultery couldn't keep you from God. You may have lied and stolen. You may have been a drug addict or an alcoholic. You did all kinds of things, yet you came to the Lord. You believed and confessed Jesus as your Lord, and instantly you came into relationship with God.

But now that you're born again, you feel guilty. You know you ought to be studying the Word more. You've made a promise to have a daily devotion time, but you haven't kept it. You got mad at your spouse on the way to church, or you had an argument and haven't been home. You didn't go to your kid's ballgame, and you feel guilty. God accepted you when you were an adulterer, liar, thief, addict, and murderer, but now, if you don't read your daily Bible readings and pray He's liable to let you die of cancer.

A Works Mentality

As ye have therefore received Christ Jesus the Lord, so walk ye in him.

Colossians 2:6

In order to receive the Lord Jesus Christ, you had to first hear about the grace of God. God commended His love toward you. While you were yet a sinner, Christ died for you. Two thousand years ago Jesus bore the sins of the world before you were ever born. When you heard the good news of the grace of God, your faith just reached out and appropriated it.

But now that you've become religious, you've started trying to earn things. You may be doing "good things" like fasting, praying, and studying the Word, but your motive is to merit God's favor. Your faith is no longer in the unconditional love of God that made everything available to you by His grace. Your focus is on how holy you're living. Your faith is in you, not grace.

Perhaps you are deflecting what I'm sharing and saying to yourself, "That's not me." Be honest with yourself before the Lord. This is where most people live. They are in a works mentality, which is why they aren't experiencing a greater relationship with God and manifesting their salvation benefits. They feel they have to earn God's provision, so they are constantly trying to perform instead of just receiving God's love by grace—putting faith in the unmerited, unearned, undeserved favor of God. God's love for you has nothing to do with how good you are.

Imagine that you're in one of my meetings right now and someone just fell over dead. I've seen three people raised from the dead, including my own son. He was dead for over five hours, but was raised up completely healed. I've seen blind eyes and deaf ears opened. I've seen cancers, AIDS, diabetes, and many other diseases healed. If I said, "All right, how many of you believe that God can raise this person from the dead?" you would be right there with me. If I continued saying, "I'm going to pray for them and we're going to see this person raised from the dead," you'd be excited, getting up out of your seat, and moving toward the front for a better look.

But I would probably lose you when I said, "All right. If you believe it, you come up here and pray for them." All of a sudden, the excitement would drain right out of you. Your faith would turn into unbelief and your anticipation into dread. It's not that you doubt God can do it. You doubt God's willingness to use His ability on your behalf because you don't feel worthy.

Independent of You

You haven't yet understood that all provision is totally based in the grace of God. You think you have to do something to merit and earn it. That's why you have more faith in my prayers than you have in your own. If you knew me as well as you know you, you wouldn't have any more faith in my prayers than you have in your prayers. It's true! You think that preachers have it all worked out and we live holy all of the time. Talk to my wife. She loves me in spite of who I am, not because of who I am.

The problem is, you know you so well you bear a sin consciousness. You feel unworthy because you don't fully understand that it's all by the grace of God. God hasn't ever had anybody qualified working for Him yet. I'm not qualified to do what I do. God doesn't use me because I'm qualified. I'm not holy enough in myself to be used of God. I have to stand up and believe in the goodness and grace of God.

This is the number one truth I've received from this revelation. I've applied it to my relationship with God, and I now know His love for me. I've experienced it. That day I realized how ungodly I was and confessed all of my sins was the first and greatest revelation I've ever had of God's love. It wasn't based on any worth or goodness of my own. It had nothing to do with me. God loves you completely independent of you. You don't have to earn or deserve this love; it's the grace of God.

God, by grace, loved you before you were born again. (Rom. 5:8.) Now that you are born again, he loves you much, much, much more. (v. 9.) Even if you are the sorriest saint you know, God loves you infinitely more than He ever loved you before you were born again. God's love for you is unconditional. It's unending and unchanging. Since you didn't do anything to cause God to love you, you can't do anything to cause Him not to love you. God's love for you has never been tied to anything you've done.

All Things

God loves you. If you could grasp this revelation, it would solve all of your problems. "But you don't understand. I'm dying. God's love wouldn't solve that problem." Yes, it would!

...faith...worketh by love.

Galatians 5:6

If you understood how much God loved you, your faith would shoot through the roof. You'd be overwhelmed! God loved you enough to bear your sins, suffer the shame, and die for you.

He that spared not his own Son, but delivered him up for us all, how shall he not with him also freely give us all things?

Romans 8:32

Compared to being forgiven and loved by God, being healed is insignificant. You may not have ever thought of it this way, but if you're struggling to believe that God is going to heal you and that you'll see that healing, you're really struggling with the love of God.

A Standstill

Once, a man brought his daughter in a wheelchair to one of our meetings. She was twelve years old and quadriplegic. Her brain was severely damaged, she couldn't talk or communicate in any way. She was totally incapacitated. She was twelve years old, but had never in her life responded to another human being. She was breathing, but she wasn't alive. This man became offended and got up, and left during the service when I declared that it is God's will for every person to be healed.

The people who brought this man to the meeting said, "Why don't you just wait until after the service is over and ask Andrew what he's talking about? Maybe he could explain it." The man stayed, and we talked afterwards. I stood in front of his daughter who was sitting in the wheelchair. He was behind the wheelchair, telling me that God had made his girl this way. This was God's will and He's getting glory out of this. This man was misinterpreting scripture.

I shared with him from James 1 that God is not the author of these things.

> Let no man say when he is tempted, I am tempted of God: for God cannot be tempted with evil, neither tempteth he any man.

> James 1:13

Every good gift and every perfect gift is from above, and cometh down from the Father of lights, with whom is no variableness, neither shadow of turning.

James 1:17

He thought I was misusing my scriptures, and I thought he was misusing his. We were at a standstill.

"What Kind of a Father Are You?"

Since this guy was already mad at me, I thought, *I have nothing to lose,* so I just looked at him and said, "What kind of a father are you in the first place? You don't even love your daughter. You don't care if she's ever normal. You don't care if she ever walks. You don't care if she ever interacts with anybody, if she ever gets married. You don't care! You don't love your daughter!"

This guy was hot! He was boiling mad, yelling at me, and saying, "I would do anything. If there was an operation, I would pay any amount of money. If I could, I would be like her so that she could be well."

Then I turned to him and said, "And you think God loves your daughter less than you do!"

We could have argued scriptures and doctrine forever, but when I brought it down to just love, he knew that there was nothing that would have kept him from ministering to his daughter and healing her if he could. Yet here he was thinking that God, who is all-powerful, didn't care about his daughter as much as he did. When I brought it down to relationship and spoke of love, he just had to say, "I see your point. If God is any kind of a God at all—any kind of a good God—it must be His will for my daughter to be well."

Chapter 18
You Qualify!

Understanding God's love would solve your theological problems. It would get rid of this thinking that God is the One causing earthquakes, hurricanes, tsunamis, tornadoes, and other bad things to happen to judge people. That's not God!

Religion has been misrepresenting the Lord. They will preach the Gospel to a degree. They sing the song, "Just as I am, without one plea," and preach grace for sinners to be born again. That's why it's so easy to be born again. Grace is presented, and faith is simply your positive response to what God has already done.

Suppose salvation had been presented differently: "Jesus might forgive your sins. He might come to this earth and die for you if you will repent and pray hard enough. If you promise never to do anything wrong again and live holy, then God might save you." You would never have gotten saved because you would have thought, *It will never work for me*. But the reason it was easy for you to receive salvation is because it was presented as already provided.

This is good news, not good prophecy. It's already happened. It has already taken place. The news is supposed to tell you about what has already happened. The reason it's easy to get born again is because you're told that Jesus already died for the sins of the world. He's already commended His love toward us in that while we were yet sinners, He died for us. It's news. So you say, "Well, if it's already happened, I'll receive it."

It's easy to reach out and receive something that's already done. If it's already done, then there's no element of doubt in it, no wondering if God will really do it. That's the reason you get born again relatively easy. But then you run into the same problem as the Galatians.

"O Foolish Galatians"

The Galatians received the Gospel and were born again, but then shortly afterwards, religious Jews came in and started saying, "Faith in Jesus isn't enough. You also have to be circumcised, keep the law, and observe the feasts. You have to start doing this and stop doing that." These religious people started perverting and changing the Gospel. They said, "You may get born again by grace, but God won't bless you, answer your prayers, or move in your life until you start living holy."

Paul responded to this perversion of the Gospel by writing his letter to the Galatians. It's his most aggressive, vicious attack on this false teaching found anywhere in the Bible!

O foolish Galatians, who hath bewitched you…?

Galatians 3:1

The word translated "foolish" literally means "stupid idiots."

Paul is saying that this teaching is demonic. He was telling them, "You're living in deception!"

> But though we, or an angel from heaven, preach any other gospel unto you than that which we have preached unto you, let him be accursed.
>
> Galatians 1:8

Some of Paul's readers must have thought, *Oh, that's too hard. He couldn't have meant that.* So the next verse says:

> As we said before, so say I now again, If any man preach any other gospel unto you than that ye have received, let him be accursed.
>
> Galatians 1:9

Paul didn't want anybody to misunderstand what he was saying or the fervency behind his words. This is where the body of Christ is today. They're preaching salvation to a degree, saying that you get born again by grace. We sing, "Just as I am without one plea," but then after you're born again, we start singing, "Just as I'm supposed to be." We're consumed with trying to live right, wondering, *Oh God. Have I done enough?*

Performance

People come up to me by the thousands saying, "Why hasn't God healed me? I fast and pray. I study the Word and pay my tithes. I attend church and read the Word. I'm doing everything I know to do.

Why hasn't God healed me?" You just told me why you aren't healed. You never pointed to what Jesus did for you. You've pointed to what you have been doing, which reveals that your faith is in all of your doing, thinking that God responds to your faith. That's not a balance of grace and faith.

Faith doesn't move God. God has provided everything for you, independent of you. All faith does is reach out and appropriate what Jesus has already done. If you're pointing to your goodness, then you aren't putting faith in God's grace. You're putting faith in your efforts and performance.

It's good for you to do all these things—pray, fast, read the Word, attend church, tithe—but don't do them to affect God. God's love for you isn't based on what you do. He didn't save you because you were worth saving. He didn't save you because of some goodness in your life. It was His grace that commended His love toward you while you were yet a sinner. Your holiness, or lack thereof, does not change God's heart toward you. God loved you before you were holy. Now that you are semi-holy, He doesn't love you any less, nor will He love you any more.

But your holiness will change *your* heart towards God. You need to study the Word to change your heart, but not because God is looking at your heart to reward you and answer your prayers now that you've been good enough. You need to attend church because it helps you. Meeting with other believers helps you as you hear the Word of God and fellowship with other people. You need to come to meetings where people are expounding the Word of God, speaking the truth, and displaying the power of God. You need to hear testimonies of people being healed, tumors being dissolved, and miracles happening. It's good for you. It helps you.

But none of this makes God love you any more. He's not keeping a record of your church attendance and you can't cash in so many meetings for one answered prayer. If you never go to church again, God would love you exactly the same, but you're foolish if you don't go to church. We're being bombarded with unbelief constantly. You need someplace where you can go hear the truth. You need to be around people who will love you and turn the other cheek when you do something wrong. You need to be in the fellowship of believers. You're foolish if you don't go to church. But God loves you anyway! His love for you is based on His grace, not your performance.

Not a Problem

I can try to have a positive self-image, thinking that I'm never wrong and everybody else is the problem. It's never me; it's always somebody else. But eventually, I just have to look in the mirror and see that I do some dumb things. I make mistakes. It blesses me to know that God's love is not conditional.

Just recently, I was sharing with my partners that we've made the biggest expansion we've ever made in our ministry. We took a huge step of faith and went on the second largest television station in America. It costs us nearly $70,000 a month to be on this station and I've been on it now for eighteen months. We've put nearly $600,000 more into this broadcast than what's come out of it, so I've had to take a step back. Some people just can't handle that. They panic at the thought of making a mistake. Well, this wouldn't be the first one I've ever made. They say, "I don't know if I can cope with that." It's not a problem for me.

Some people think that when God touches your life, you immediately become perfect. That's not been my experience at all. It's more like this: I'm moving in the direction that God wants me to go, but I'm not doing everything perfectly. God could have picked somebody better than me. He could have chosen someone with a much better grasp of the English language and much more charisma than I have. I'm definitely not the sharpest knife in the drawer, but praise God, I'm seeing good things happen just because I know that God loves me in spite of me and not because of me.

There are very few "perfect" people who think they are the greatest. Most of us deal with feelings of unworthiness and wonder, *God, why did You choose me? I'm not qualified.* If you follow people in the Bible, you'll see that every person the Lord called, said, "God, I can't do it!" They struggled for a period of time.

> *For ye see your calling, brethren, how that not many wise men after the flesh, not many mighty, not many noble, are called: But God hath chosen the foolish things of the world to confound the wise; and God hath chosen the weak things of the world to confound the things which are mighty; and base things of the world, and things which are despised, hath God chosen, yea, and things which are not, to bring to nought things that are: That no flesh should glory in his*

presence. But of him are ye in Christ Jesus, who of God is made unto us wisdom, and righteousness, and sanctification, and redemption.

1 Corinthians 1:26–30

God has not chosen many mighty or noble people who just have it all together. God chooses the base things of the world, things that are despised and things that are nothing, to bring to naught things that are.

Apply Within

If you're a loser, a nothing—you qualify to be used of God! God isn't against people who have all of these great abilities and talents, it's just that all of your abilities and talents compared to God's are nothing. You have to come to the end of yourself and say, "Oh Lord, it's got to be You." God says, "If you're a nothing, if you are base, if you're despised—apply within." You must come to the end of yourself and realize that it's not about you.

When you understand grace, you recognize that it's not based on any goodness of your own. It's just based on God's love. He loves you in spite of who you are, not because of who you are. God loved you before you were born. He loved you before you sinned. He loved you even after you had sinned. He commended His love towards you. Now that you've accepted Him, He loves you even more than He ever loved you before because now you have made Jesus your Lord. You are a part of Him. The grace—the blessing—of God is in your life unconditionally.

That's what I received from that experience in 1968. For the first time in my life, I saw that I was a zero with the rim knocked off. I had no confidence in and no satisfaction with myself, whatsoever. Upon this recognition of my worst state, God's love flowed into me. I just knew His love had nothing to do with me. I knew that God loved me because He is love. That's what changed my life.

Chapter 19

Forgiven

⟬∼⟭

God manifested His love toward us in that He died for us while we were yet sinners. (Rom. 5:8.) Yet through religion, the devil has convinced us that God's love, acceptance, and favor toward us is tied to our works and performance. You believe God exists. You know He is able. You just doubt His willingness to move in your behalf because you feel condemned over your sins.

For more on this subject, read these books: *The War Is Over, Redemption,* and *Spirit, Soul & Body.* They all deal with these truths more thoroughly than I'm able to here.

Most people think that God offers you forgiveness of all your sins committed up until the time you become born again. When you accept Jesus, your past sins are forgiven, but then every sin you commit after that has to be dealt with, repented of, and put back under the blood. There are primarily two versions of this. The extreme version says that if you have a sin in your life that isn't confessed and you were to die in a car wreck before you got that sin confessed, you would go to hell. Even though you might have been born again for twenty years, if you have an unconfessed sin in your life when you die, you go to hell. You lose your salvation even though you've walked with God for many years. Most Christians believe a lesser interpretation of the same principle. They say that God won't answer your prayer, fellowship with, or use you if there's any sin in your life. Both versions of this are wrong.

Missing the Mark

According to Hebrews 9, 10, and 12, God forgave all of your sins—past, present, and future. Even sins you haven't committed yet have already been forgiven. Your salvation, God's love for you, His willingness to use you and answer your prayers are not dependent upon you getting every sin confessed. If it were, the moment you became born again you should hope to die immediately because that's the only way you could be certain of going to heaven. If this line of thinking were true, you could never walk in the joy of the Lord. Why? Because sin isn't only the wrong things you do. The Bible says:

> *Therefore to him that knoweth to do good, and doeth it not, to him it is sin.*
>
> James 4:17

Sin is also what you should be doing but you're failing to do.

Every believer should love their spouse the way that Christ loved the Church. You might be doing better at loving your spouse than you've ever done, but you aren't doing it perfectly. Every believer is supposed to reverence their spouse the way that the Church should reverence Christ. You might be reverencing your spouse better than other people, but no one reverences their spouse the way that the Church is supposed to reverence Christ. None of us studies the Word as much as we would like to and know that we should. No one operates in love towards others exactly the way that we should. Nobody's perfect. You commit sins that you aren't even aware of. You fail all of the time. According to the Bible, sin is missing the mark. We're all missing the mark. If you think that you have to have every sin confessed before God will act, just give it up. You're never going to get there.

You may say, "According to 1 John 1:9, aren't we supposed to confess our sin?" I strongly recommend that you check out my book entitled *The War Is Over.* I devoted an entire chapter to answering that very question. I'll provide a brief summary of that answer here.

All of your sin—past, present, and even the ones you haven't committed yet—have already been forgiven. (Heb. 9, 10, 12.) The instant you were born again, your new man, your born-again spirit, was created in righteousness and true holiness. (Eph. 4:24.) You were sanctified and perfected forever. (Heb. 10:10,14.) In that same moment, you were sealed by the Holy Spirit. (Eph. 1:13.) When you sin, sin doesn't penetrate that seal around your spirit. It doesn't get in and affect your spirit. Since God is a Spirit, He sees you, Spirit to born-again spirit. (John 4:24.) This means God sees you as righteous, holy, and pure as Jesus is. (1 Cor. 6:17; 1 John 4:17.) That's the way your born-again spirit is, and it's sealed. When you sin, that sin doesn't affect your right standing with God. It's through who you are in Christ—your born-again spirit—that you must fellowship with God.

Drive Satan Out

However, your body and soul get defiled when you sin. Satan comes only to steal, kill, and destroy. (John 10:10.) If you yield to sin, you're yielding yourself to the author of that sin—the devil. (Rom. 6:16.) Yielding to sin gives Satan an inroad into your physical body to bring poverty, sickness, and disease. It gives him an inroad into your soul to bring depression, discouragement, and the like. So yes, sin still has consequences—but not on your born-again spirit or your relationship with God. It's your soul and body that get contaminated and defiled. If you give Satan an inroad into your life, he'll work to destroy you in the only ways he can.

So as a believer, what do we do when we know that we've sinned? First of all, if you are walking in the knowledge and revelation that God has given you, then the blood of Christ cleanses you from the sins that you don't even know about.

If we walk in the light, as he is in the light, we have fellowship one with another, and the blood of Jesus Christ his Son cleanseth us from all sin.

1 John 1:7

But when you do know that you've committed a sin, 1 John 1:9 says to confess it.

If we confess our sins, he is faithful and just to forgive us our sins, and to cleanse us from all unrighteousness.

1 John 1:9

Confess means to acknowledge your sin to God.[1] You're saying, "God, You were right. I was wrong. I turn from this sin." By confessing and repenting, you're closing the door on the devil. You're also drawing out into your flesh (body and soul) the righteousness and holiness that already exist in your born-again spirit. This will drive Satan out of your life. Even though you gave the devil a legal right to come into your life by yielding to sin, when you confess, repent, and turn from it, you give this power that is located in your spirit the ability to come out and cleanse you from all unrighteousness.

Never Fluctuated

First John 1:9 doesn't mean that you must confess every sin in order to have relationship with God. That would be impossible. You don't even realize every time you sin! If I've rubbed some of your religious traditions the wrong way, you may be sinning against me right now. You could be thinking some evil thoughts toward me. But whether you like it or not, I'm your brother in the Lord. Who knows, perhaps we'll be neighbors in heaven. If you're hating me in your heart, the Bible says that you are guilty of murder. (1 John 3:15.)

You can't live this way. Even if you aren't offended at me, some day you'll be offended with someone. Thinking that you have to keep everything confessed in order to be right with God puts the burden of salvation on you. You might as well try to save yourself. No, there's

---

[1] http://www.merriam-webster.com/dictionary/confess, s.v. "confess."

only one Savior, and you're not Him! Jesus died for all of your sins—past, present, and even future sins. You are forgiven.

You need to understand that there's nothing you've done that made God love you. There's nothing you can do that will make God not love you. He is love. (1 John 4:8.) However, there are lots of things you can do that will keep you from full understanding of the truth. Sin will make you spiritually retarded. Your heart will become hardened, cold, insensitive, unyielding, and unfeeling toward God. (Heb. 3:13.)

Sin isn't smart. It's foolish. It's an emotional response. When you sin, you put blinders on. You can't see or perceive. You become dull and lose your perception. Yes, sin has consequences. But God is a Spirit, and He's looking at you in the spirit. (John 4:24.) Even when you've sinned and given Satan an inroad into your life, God's love for you has never fluctuated. He loves you just as much as He ever did. He doesn't love you because you're lovely. He loves you because He is love.

Sober, Righteous, and Holy

You may be thinking that I'm encouraging you to sin. No, I'm not! I hate sin. You can't say, "Andrew, you preach grace because it allows you to go live in sin." I've lived holier accidentally than most people have ever lived on purpose. My standard of holiness is much stricter than the vast majority of people. A true understanding of God's grace does not encourage sin.

Forgiven

For the grace of God that bringeth salvation hath appeared to all men, teaching us that, denying ungodliness and worldly lusts, we should live soberly, righteously, and godly, in this present world.

Titus 2:11–12

The grace of God teaches you to live a sober, righteous, and holy life. The grace of God hasn't caused me to go live in sin. You're mistaken if you think that I'm encouraging people to live in sin. I'm encouraging people to understand that God's love for them is unconditional. And if you ever get a revelation of that, you'll serve God more accidentally than you ever have on purpose.

Chapter 20

Religion or Relationship?

Love will be a greater motivation to serve God than fear ever was. Fear has torment. (1 John 4:18.) Many Christians are tormented in their relationship with God thinking, *I have to do all these things in order for God to love me.*

What kind of a relationship would you have if your spouse came up to you and said, "All right, unless you do this, that, and the other, I'm not going to fellowship with you. I'm keeping a checklist, and the first time you get out of line, I'm not going to talk to you. You aren't getting any money from me. I'm going to punish you."

That's how religion has presented God. "He's not going to talk to you. He won't answer your prayers, or even listen to them. God has His fingers in His ears until you repent. He'll throw a fit and a temper tantrum. He's liable to strike your child dead because He's displeased that you haven't read your daily Bible readings." No one wants to live with a person like that!

You can't have a good relationship with God if you're basing it upon your performance and fear. This is the picture that religion has painted of God, and we wonder why people are struggling to maintain a relationship.

My Favorite Thing to Do

God loves you because He's a good God. It's grace, and your faith doesn't move Him. God isn't responding to you. Your faith is a response to Him. You need to understand that God loves you and deals with you by grace. He's already forgiven all of your sins. You need to quit sinning so that you don't let Satan have an inroad into your life. But your holiness—or lack thereof—is not the basis of your relationship with God.

By understanding and applying these truths to your life, you'll move to a whole new level of relationship with God. It should be so easy to believe Him. If God loved you enough to die for you while you were an absolute enemy of the cross, how much more does He love you now that you're just His imperfect child? How much more does He want to move in your life now? This knowledge reduces the Christian life down to where it's simple, as God intended it to be.

God loves me. I study the Word, not to get God to love me, but because I want to read His love letter and discover how much He loves me. I pray, not because I have to, but because I want to. I'm not just punching a time clock and getting my "credit." I pray because I love God and truly enjoy hanging out with Him.

Religion or Relationship?

The worship leaders of our citywide meetings often sing a song that says, "My favorite thing to do is to spend my time with You." Is this true of you? Is spending time with God truly your favorite activity? It is for me. I don't share this to build myself up and put you down. I share it to encourage you to know that it's possible. In fact, this kind of intimacy and relationship with God isn't just possible—it's what He created us for in the first place.

What religion and tradition have taught you about God hinders you from enjoying Him. It's not easy to hang out with somebody you think is killing babies, making some retarded, and causing others to be born deformed. How can you draw near to someone who "sent" the terrorist attacks, violent weather, and other so-called "acts of God"? You can't. But when you understand the truth of how good God really is, your favorite thing to do will be just to love and hang out with Him.

A Free Gift

I say this with love and compassion, but if this isn't your experience—then you're religious. You've been deceived. You're putting faith in your effort and thinking that God is responding to you. You need to understand God's grace and that your faith is simply how you appropriate the goodness of God. I'm sure this is challenging much of what you've believed, but it's true.

Perhaps in the course of reading this book, you've realized that your faith has been in your own works and performance instead of in Christ.

I'd like to give you an opportunity to begin a true relationship with God. However, you need to understand that you don't become a Christian by being born into a "Christian" nation or by growing up in a Christian home. Attending church doesn't make you a Christian any more than sitting in a garage would make you a car. You must be born again.

You must come to the end of trusting in yourself and understand that God loves you—not because you deserve it, but because He is love. He sent His Son, Jesus Christ, two thousand years ago to pay for all of your sins. That payment has already been made. Will you accept it now as a free gift?

> *If thou shalt confess with thy mouth the Lord Jesus, and shalt believe in thine heart that God hath raised him from the dead, thou shalt be saved.*
>
> Romans 10:9

The Bible way to receive this gift of salvation is to confess with your mouth that Jesus is Lord and to believe in your heart that God raised Him from the dead. If you do, you'll be saved. But making Jesus your Lord is more than just saying those words. You have to be willing to submit to Jesus as your Lord. That means He's in control and not you. I'm not saying you will do all this perfectly, but you have to be willing for that to happen.

Make Jesus Your Lord

You might be religious. You might be a good person, thinking, *Well, I'm good enough. God will accept me.* It's not about your goodness or what you have or haven't done. It's about what Jesus did. You have to humble yourself and receive salvation as a gift. If you've never done this before, I encourage you to make Jesus your Lord right now.

You could pray from your heart something like this:

Jesus, I turn from trusting in myself and my own works for salvation. I confess that You are my Lord. I believe in my heart that God raised You from the dead, and I receive Your gift of salvation right now by faith. Thank You for revealing Your love and grace to me!

Once you're born again, you also need the baptism in the Holy Spirit. The truths I've shared from God's Word in this book won't be understandable to someone who is just operating out of their own intellect. You must have the Holy Spirit give you revelation of what I've been talking about.

The Number One Benefit

I quit arguing with people a long time ago. When I first started out in ministry, I used to argue with people. I'd fight with them, using lots of scripture, trying to convince them of the truth. I don't do that anymore. I've realized that understanding the truth must come by revelation. And that's the job of the Holy Spirit. (John 14:26; 16:13.)

Revelation knowledge is the number one benefit of receiving the baptism in the Holy Spirit. The very Person who inspired the Bible will begin teaching you what it says. As you pray in tongues, the Word says that you are praying the hidden wisdom of God. (1 Cor. 14:2; 2:7.) Then you can pray to interpret that tongue. (1 Cor. 14:13.) This is how you can receive revelation knowledge.

This is how God showed me most of these truths I've shared in this book. I put the truth in me by reading and studying God's Word, but I couldn't understand it. So I prayed in tongues and believed for the interpretation. God would then give me the revelation and explain to me what it meant. It's my personal conviction from both God's Word and my experience that you just can't understand many of the things of God without the quickening power of the Holy Spirit.

If the Bible seems like a closed book to you, it's because the Holy Spirit wrote it to your heart—not your brain. You need to get the Author of the Bible to reveal its truths to you. Although praying in tongues is important as it comes as a part of the baptism in the Holy Spirit "package," the number one benefit I experienced when I received the Holy Spirit was revelation knowledge. I began to understand. Revelation knowledge just exploded on the inside of me.

Once you're born again, you need to be baptized in the Holy Spirit. You need this in order to succeed in the Christian life, to operate in the gifts of the Holy Spirit, and to go on in the things of God. As His child, your loving heavenly Father wants to give you the supernatural power you need to live this new life. If you haven't already done so, I encourage you to receive this gift—the baptism in the Holy Spirit—right now.

Receive the Holy Spirit

All you have to do to receive the baptism in the Holy Spirit is ask, believe, and receive.

> *For every one that asketh receiveth; and he that seeketh findeth; and to him that knocketh it shall be opened...how much more shall your heavenly Father give the Holy Spirit to them that ask him?*
>
> Luke 11:10,13

Go ahead and pray from your heart something like this:

Father, I recognize my need for Your power to understand Your Word and to live this new life. I desire to receive Your revelation knowledge. Please fill me with Your Holy Spirit. By faith, I receive it right now. Thank You for baptizing me. Holy Spirit, You are welcome in my life!

Congratulations—now you're filled with God's supernatural power!

Some syllables from a language you don't recognize will rise up from your heart to your mouth. (1 Cor. 14:14.) As you speak them out loud by faith, you're releasing God's power from within and building yourself up in the spirit. (1 Cor. 14:4.) You can do this whenever and wherever you like!

It doesn't really matter whether you felt anything or not when you prayed to receive the Lord and His Spirit. If you believed in your heart that you received, then God's Word promises that you did.

Therefore I say unto you, What things soever ye desire, when ye pray, believe that ye receive them, and ye shall have them.

Mark 11:24

God always honors His Word—believe it!

Please contact me and let me know that you've prayed to receive Jesus as your Lord and/or to be filled with the Holy Spirit. I would like to rejoice with you and help you understand more fully what has taken place in your life. I'll send you a free book entitled, *The New You & the Holy Spirit,* which explains salvation and the baptism of the Holy Spirit. It's the same book I give to everyone who comes forward to receive these gifts at our meetings. Thousands of people have received the gift of speaking in tongues by reading this book. We have a Helpline staffed by mature Christians who will be glad to pray with you. Our Helpline is open from 4:00 A.M. to 9:30 P.M. (Mountain Time) each weekday. The number is (719) 635-1111. Give us a call—we're here to help you understand and grow in your new relationship with the Lord.

Welcome to your new life. May you enjoy an intimate relationship with God as you live each day in the balance of grace and faith!

Grace and Faith Scriptures

But now the righteousness of God without the law is manifested, being witnessed by the law and the prophets; even the righteousness of God *which is* by faith of Jesus Christ unto all and upon all them that believe: for there is no difference: For all have sinned, and come short of the glory of God; being justified freely by his grace through the redemption that is in Christ Jesus: Whom God hath set forth *to be* a propitiation through faith in his blood, to declare his righteousness for the remission of sins that are past, through the forbearance of God; to declare, *I say,* at this time his righteousness: that he might be just, and the justifier of him which believeth in Jesus.

Romans 3:21–26

Therefore *it is* of faith, that *it might be* by grace; to the end the promise might be sure to all the seed; not to that only which is of the law, but to that also which is of the faith of Abraham; who is the father of us all.

Romans 4:16

By whom also we have access by faith into this grace wherein we stand, and rejoice in hope of the glory of God.

Romans 5:2

For I say, through the grace given unto me, to every man that is among you, not to think *of himself* more highly than he ought to think; but to think soberly, according as God hath dealt to every man the measure of faith.

Romans 12:3

Having then gifts differing according to the grace that is given to us, whether prophecy, *let us prophesy* according to the proportion of faith.

Romans 12:6

Therefore, as ye abound in every *thing, in* faith, and utterance, and knowledge, and *in* all diligence, and *in* your love to us, *see* that ye abound in this grace also.

2 Corinthians 8:7

For by grace are ye saved through faith; and that not of yourselves: *it is* the gift of God.

Ephesians 2:8

And the grace of our Lord was exceeding abundant with faith and love which is in Christ Jesus.

1 Timothy 1:14

Grace Scriptures

And the Word was made flesh, and dwelt among us, (and we beheld his glory, the glory as of the only begotten of the Father,) full of grace and truth.

John 1:14

For the law was given by Moses, *but* grace and truth came by Jesus Christ.

John 1:17

Long time therefore abode they speaking boldly in the Lord, which gave testimony unto the word of his grace, and granted signs and wonders to be done by their hands.

Acts 14:3

But we believe that through the grace of the Lord Jesus Christ we shall be saved, even as they.

Acts 15:11

But none of these things move me, neither count I my life dear unto myself, so that I might finish my course with joy, and the ministry, which I have received of the Lord Jesus, to testify the gospel of the grace of God.

Acts 20:24

And now, brethren, I commend you to God, and to the word of his grace, which is able to build you up, and to give you an inheritance among all them which are sanctified.

Acts 20:32

But not as the offence, so also *is* the free gift. For if through the offence of one many be dead, much more the grace of God, and the gift by grace, *which is* by one man, Jesus Christ, hath abounded unto many.

Romans 5:15

Moreover the law entered, that the offence might abound. But where sin abounded, grace did much more abound: That as sin hath reigned unto death, even so might grace reign through righteousness unto eternal life by Jesus Christ our Lord.

Romans 5:20–21

For sin shall not have dominion over you: for ye are not under the law, but under grace.

Romans 6:14

What then? shall we sin, because we are not under the law, but under grace? God forbid. Know ye not, that to whom ye yield yourselves servants to obey, his servants ye are to whom ye obey; whether of sin unto death, or of obedience unto righteousness?

Romans 6:15–16

And if by grace, then *is it* no more of works: otherwise grace is no more grace. But if *it be* of works, then is it no more grace: otherwise work is no more work.

Romans 11:6

According to the grace of God which is given unto me, as a wise masterbuilder, I have laid the foundation, and another buildeth thereon. But let every man take heed how he buildeth thereupon.

1 Corinthians 3:10

But by the grace of God I am what I am: and his grace which *was bestowed* upon me was not in vain; but I laboured more abundantly than they all: yet not I, but the grace of God which was with me.

1 Corinthians 15:10

For all things *are* for your sakes, that the abundant grace might through the thanksgiving of many redound to the glory of God.

2 Corinthians 4:15

We then, *as* workers together *with him,* beseech *you* also that ye receive not the grace of God in vain.

2 Corinthians 6:1

For ye know the grace of our Lord Jesus Christ, that, though he was rich, yet for your sakes he became poor, that ye through his poverty might be rich.

2 Corinthians 8:9

And God *is* able to make all grace abound toward you; that ye, always having all sufficiency in all *things,* may abound to every good work.

2 Corinthians 9:8

And he said unto me, My grace is sufficient for thee: for my strength is made perfect in weakness. Most gladly therefore will I rather glory in my infirmities, that the power of Christ may rest upon me.

2 Corinthians 12:9

I do not frustrate the grace of God: for if righteousness *come* by the law, then Christ is dead in vain.

Galatians 2:21

Christ is become of no effect unto you, whosoever of you are justified by the law; ye are fallen from grace.

Galatians 5:4

To the praise of the glory of his grace, wherein he hath made us accepted in the beloved.

Ephesians 1:6

In whom we have redemption through his blood, the forgiveness of sins, according to the riches of his grace; wherein he hath abounded toward us in all wisdom and prudence; having made known unto us the mystery of his will, according to his good pleasure which he hath purposed in himself.

Ephesians 1:7-9

But unto every one of us is given grace according to the measure of the gift of Christ.

Ephesians 4:7

Let no corrupt communication proceed out of your mouth, but that which is good to the use of edifying, that it may minister grace unto the hearers.

Ephesians 4:29

Let the word of Christ dwell in you richly in all wisdom; teaching and admonishing one another in psalms and hymns and spiritual songs, singing with grace in your hearts to the Lord.

Colossians 3:16

Let your speech *be* always with grace, seasoned with salt, that ye may know how ye ought to answer every man.

Colossians 4:6

For the grace of God that bringeth salvation hath appeared to all men, Teaching us that, denying ungodliness and worldly lusts, we should live soberly, righteously, and godly, in this present world.

Titus 2:11–12

Not by works of righteousness which we have done, but according to his mercy he saved us, by the washing of regeneration, and renewing of the Holy Ghost; which he shed on us abundantly through Jesus Christ our Saviour; that being justified by his grace, we should be made heirs according to the hope of eternal life.

Titus 3:5–7

But we see Jesus, who was made a little lower than the angels for the suffering of death, crowned with glory and honour; that he by the grace of God should taste death for every man.

Hebrews 2:9

Let us therefore come boldly unto the throne of grace, that we may obtain mercy, and find grace to help in time of need.

Hebrews 4:16

Wherefore we receiving a kingdom which cannot be moved, let us have grace, whereby we may serve God acceptably with reverence and godly fear: For our God is a consuming fire.

Hebrews 12:28–29

Be not carried about with divers and strange doctrines. For it is a good thing that the heart be established with grace; not with meats, which have not profited them that have been occupied therein.

Hebrews 13:9

But he giveth more grace. Wherefore he saith, God resisteth the proud, but giveth grace unto the humble.

James 4:6

Likewise, ye husbands, dwell with *them* according to knowledge, giving honour unto the wife, as unto the weaker vessel, and as being heirs together of the grace of life; that your prayers be not hindered.

1 Peter 3:7

As every man hath received the gift, *even so* minister the same one to another, as good stewards of the manifold grace of God.

1 Peter 4:10

Likewise, ye younger, submit yourselves unto the elder. Yea, all *of you* be subject one to another, and be clothed with humility: for God resisteth the proud, and giveth grace to the humble.

1 Peter 5:5

The grace of our Lord Jesus Christ *be* with you all. Amen.

Revelation 22:21

Faith Scriptures

Wherefore, if God so clothe the grass of the field, which to day is, and to morrow is cast into the oven, *shall he* not much more *clothe* you, O ye of little faith?

Matthew 6:30

When Jesus heard *it,* he marvelled, and said to them that followed, Verily I say unto you, I have not found so great faith, no, not in Israel.

Matthew 8:10

And he saith unto them, Why are ye fearful, O ye of little faith? Then he arose, and rebuked the winds and the sea; and there was a great calm.

Matthew 8:26

And, behold, they brought to him a man sick of the palsy, lying on a bed: and Jesus seeing their faith said unto the sick of the palsy; Son, be of good cheer; thy sins be forgiven thee.

Matthew 9:2

But Jesus turned him about, and when he saw her, he said, Daughter, be of good comfort; thy faith hath made thee whole. And the woman was made whole from that hour.

Matthew 9:22

Then Jesus answered and said unto her, O woman, great *is* thy faith: be it unto thee even as thou wilt. And her daughter was made whole from that very hour.

Matthew 15:28

And Jesus said unto them, Because of your unbelief: for verily I say unto you, If ye have faith as a grain of mustard seed, ye shall say unto this mountain, Remove hence to yonder place; and it shall remove; and nothing shall be impossible unto you.

Matthew 17:20

Jesus answered and said unto them, Verily I say unto you, If ye have faith, and doubt not, ye shall not only do this *which is done* to the fig tree, but also if ye shall say unto this mountain, Be thou removed, and be thou cast into the sea; it shall be done.

Matthew 21:21

And Jesus said unto him, Go thy way; thy faith hath made thee whole. And immediately he received his sight, and followed Jesus in the way.

Mark 10:52

And Jesus answering saith unto them, Have faith in God.

Mark 11:22

And when he saw their faith, he said unto him, Man, thy sins are forgiven thee.

Luke 5:20

And Stephen, full of faith and power, did great wonders and miracles among the people.

Acts 6:8

The same heard Paul speak: who stedfastly beholding him, and perceiving that he had faith to be healed, said with a loud voice, Stand upright on thy feet. And he leaped and walked.

Acts 14:9–10

And as they went through the cities, they delivered them the decrees for to keep, that were ordained of the apostles and elders which were at Jerusalem. And so were the churches established in the faith, and increased in number daily.

Acts 16:4–5

And how I kept back nothing that was profitable *unto you,* but have shown you, and have taught you publicly, and from house to house, testifying both to the Jews, and also to the Greeks, repentance toward God, and faith toward our Lord Jesus Christ.

Acts 20:20–21

And I said, Who art thou, Lord? And he said, I am Jesus whom thou persecutest. But rise, and stand upon thy feet: for I have appeared unto thee for this purpose, to make thee a minister and a witness both of these things which thou hast seen, and of those things in the which I will appear unto thee…To open their eyes, *and* to turn *them* from darkness to light, and *from* the power of Satan unto God, that they may receive forgiveness of sins, and inheritance among them which are sanctified by faith that is in me.

Acts 26:15–16,18

First, I thank my God through Jesus Christ for you all, that your faith is spoken of throughout the whole world.

Romans 1:8

For therein is the righteousness of God revealed from faith to faith: as it is written, The just shall live by faith.

Romans 1:17

For what if some did not believe? shall their unbelief make the faith of God without effect? God forbid: yea, let God be true, but every man a liar; as it is written, That thou mightest be justified in thy sayings, and mightest overcome when thou art judged.

Romans 3:3–4

Where *is* boasting then? It is excluded. By what law? of works? Nay: but by the law of faith.

Romans 3:27

Therefore we conclude that a man is justified by faith without the deeds of the law.

Romans 3:28

Do we then make void the law through faith? God forbid: yea, we establish the law.

Romans 3:31

For the promise, that he should be the heir of the world, *was* not to Abraham, or to his seed, through the law, but through the righteousness of faith.

Romans 4:13

And being not weak in faith, he considered not his own body now dead, when he was about an hundred years old, neither yet the deadness of Sarah's womb: He staggered not at the promise of God through unbelief; but was strong in faith, giving glory to God.

Romans 4:19–20

Therefore being justified by faith, we have peace with God through our Lord Jesus Christ: By whom also we have access by faith into this grace wherein we stand, and rejoice in hope of the glory of God.

Romans 5:1–2

But what saith it? The word is nigh thee, *even* in thy mouth, and in thy heart: that is, the word of faith, which we preach; That if thou shalt confess with thy mouth the Lord Jesus, and shalt believe in thine heart that God hath raised him from the dead, thou shalt be saved.

Romans 10:8–9

So then faith *cometh* by hearing, and hearing by the word of God.

Romans 10:17

Hast thou faith? have *it* to thyself before God. Happy *is* he that condemneth not himself in that thing which he alloweth.

Romans 14:22

And he that doubteth is damned if he eat, because *he eateth* not of faith: for whatsoever *is* not of faith is sin.

Romans 14:23

And my speech and my preaching was not with enticing words of man's wisdom, but in demonstration of the Spirit and of power: That your faith should not stand in the wisdom of men, but in the power of God.

1 Corinthians 2:4–5

For to one is given by the Spirit the word of wisdom; to another the word of knowledge by the same Spirit; to another faith by the same Spirit; to another the gifts of healing by the same Spirit; to another the working of miracles; to another prophecy; to another discerning of spirits; to another *divers* kinds of tongues; to another the interpretation of tongues: But all these worketh that one and the selfsame Spirit, dividing to every man severally as he will.

1 Corinthians 12:8–11

And though I have *the gift of* prophecy, and understand all mysteries, and all knowledge; and though I have all faith, so that I could remove mountains, and have not charity, I am nothing.

1 Corinthians 13:2

And now abideth faith, hope, charity, these three; but the greatest of these *is* charity.

1 Corinthians 13:13

And if Christ be not risen, then *is* our preaching vain, and your faith *is* also vain.

1 Corinthians 15:14

Watch ye, stand fast in the faith, quit you like men, be strong.

1 Corinthians 16:13

Not for that we have dominion over your faith, but are helpers of your joy: for by faith ye stand.

2 Corinthians 1:24

Therefore *we are* always confident, knowing that, whilst we are at home in the body, we are absent from the Lord: (For we walk by faith, not by sight).

2 Corinthians 5:6–7

Examine yourselves, whether ye be in the faith; prove your own selves. Know ye not your own selves, how that Jesus Christ is in you, except ye be reprobates?

2 Corinthians 13:5

Knowing that a man is not justified by the works of the law, but by the faith of Jesus Christ, even we have believed in Jesus Christ, that we might be justified by the faith of Christ, and not by the works of the law: for by the works of the law shall no flesh be justified.

Galatians 2:16

I am crucified with Christ: nevertheless I live; yet not I, but Christ liveth in me: and the life which I now live in the flesh I live by the faith of the Son of God, who loved me, and gave himself for me.

Galatians 2:20

Know ye therefore that they which are of faith, the same are the children of Abraham.

Galatians 3:7

And the scripture, foreseeing that God would justify the heathen through faith, preached before the gospel unto Abraham, *saying,* In thee shall all nations be blessed. So then they which be of faith are blessed with faithful Abraham.

Galatians 3:8–9

But that no man is justified by the law in the sight of God, *it is* evident: for, The just shall live by faith.

Galatians 3:11

Christ hath redeemed us from the curse of the law, being made a curse for us: for it is written, Cursed *is* every one that hangeth on a tree: That the blessing of Abraham might come on the Gentiles through Jesus Christ; that we might receive the promise of the Spirit through faith.

Galatians 3:13–14

But the scripture hath concluded all under sin, that the promise by faith of Jesus Christ might be given to them that believe.

Galatians 3:22

But before faith came, we were kept under the law, shut up unto the faith which should afterwards be revealed. Wherefore the law was our schoolmaster *to bring us* unto Christ, that we might be justified by faith. But after that faith is come, we are no longer under a schoolmaster. For ye are all the children of God by faith in Christ Jesus.

Galatians 3:23–26

For we through the Spirit wait for the hope of righteousness by faith.

Galatians 5:5

But the fruit of the Spirit is love, joy, peace, longsuffering, gentleness, goodness, faith, meekness, temperance: against such there is no law.

Galatians 5:22–23

As we have therefore opportunity, let us do good unto all *men,* especially unto them who are of the household of faith.

Galatians 6:10

For this cause I bow my knees unto the Father of our Lord Jesus Christ…That he would grant you, according to the riches of his glory, to be strengthened with might by his Spirit in the inner man; that Christ may dwell in your hearts by faith; that ye, being rooted and grounded in love.

Ephesians 3:14,16–17

There is one body, and one Spirit, even as ye are called in one hope of your calling; one Lord, one faith, one baptism, one God and Father of all, who *is* above all, and through all, and in you all.

Ephesians 4:4–6

And he gave some, apostles; and some, prophets; and some, evangelists; and some, pastors and teachers; for the perfecting of the saints, for the work of the ministry, for the edifying of the body of Christ: Till we all come in the unity of the faith, and of the knowledge of the Son of God, unto a perfect man, unto the measure of the stature of the fulness of Christ.

Ephesians 4:11–13

Above all, taking the shield of faith, wherewith ye shall be able to quench all the fiery darts of the wicked.

Ephesians 6:16

Only let your conversation be as it becometh the gospel of Christ: that whether I come and see you, or else be absent, I may hear of your affairs, that ye stand fast in one spirit, with one mind striving together for the faith of the gospel.

Philippians 1:27

And be found in him, not having mine own righteousness, which is of the law, but that which is through the faith of Christ, the righteousness which is of God by faith.

Philippians 3:9

For though I be absent in the flesh, yet am I with you in the spirit, joying and beholding your order, and the stedfastness of your faith in Christ.

Colossians 2:5

As ye have therefore received Christ Jesus the Lord, *so* walk ye in him: Rooted and built up in him, and stablished in the faith, as ye have been taught, abounding therein with thanksgiving.

Colossians 2:6–7

Buried with him in baptism, wherein also ye are risen with *him* through the faith of the operation of God, who hath raised him from the dead.

Colossians 2:12

But let us, who are of the day, be sober, putting on the breastplate of faith and love; and for an helmet, the hope of salvation.

1 Thessalonians 5:8

Wherefore also we pray always for you, that our God would count you worthy of *this* calling, and fulfil all the good pleasure of *his* goodness, and the work of faith with power.

2 Thessalonians 1:11

Finally, brethren, pray for us, that the word of the Lord may have *free* course, and be glorified, even as *it is* with you: And that we may be delivered from unreasonable and wicked men: for all *men* have not faith.

2 Thessalonians 3:1–2

Likewise *must* the deacons *be* grave, not doubletongued, not given to much wine, not greedy of filthy lucre; holding the mystery of the faith in a pure conscience.

1 Timothy 3:8–9

Now the Spirit speaketh expressly, that in the latter times some shall depart from the faith, giving heed to seducing spirits, and doctrines of devils.

1 Timothy 4:1

For every creature of God *is* good, and nothing to be refused, if it be received with thanksgiving: For it is sanctified by the word of God and prayer. If thou put the brethren in remembrance of these things, thou shalt be a good minister of Jesus Christ, nourished up in the words of faith and of good doctrine, whereunto thou hast attained.

1 Timothy 4:4–6

Let no man despise thy youth; but be thou an example of the believers, in word, in conversation, in charity, in spirit, in faith, in purity.

1 Timothy 4:12

But if any provide not for his own, and specially for those of his own house, he hath denied the faith, and is worse than an infidel.

1 Timothy 5:8

For the love of money is the root of all evil: which while some coveted after, they have erred from the faith, and pierced themselves through with many sorrows. But thou, O man of God, flee these things; and follow after righteousness, godliness, faith, love, patience, meekness.

1 Timothy 6:10–11

Fight the good fight of faith, lay hold on eternal life, whereunto thou art also called, and hast professed a good profession before many witnesses.

1 Timothy 6:12

Flee also youthful lusts: but follow righteousness, faith, charity, peace, with them that call on the Lord out of a pure heart.

2 Timothy 2:22

But continue thou in the things which thou hast learned and hast been assured of, knowing of whom thou hast learned *them;* and that from a child thou hast known the holy scriptures, which are able to make thee wise unto salvation through faith which is in Christ Jesus.

2 Timothy 3:14–15

I have fought a good fight, I have finished *my* course, I have kept the faith: Henceforth there is laid up for me a crown of righteousness, which the Lord, the righteous judge, shall give me at that day: and not to me only, but unto all them also that love his appearing.

2 Timothy 4:7–8

For unto us was the gospel preached, as well as unto them: but the word preached did not profit them, not being mixed with faith in them that heard *it.*

Hebrews 4:2

And we desire that every one of you do shew the same diligence to the full assurance of hope unto the end: That ye be not slothful, but followers of them who through faith and patience inherit the promises.

Hebrew 6:11–12

Let us draw near with a true heart in full assurance of faith, having our hearts sprinkled from an evil conscience, and our bodies washed with pure water.

Hebrews 10:22

Let us hold fast the profession of *our* faith without wavering; (for he *is* faithful that promised).

Hebrews 10:23

Now the just shall live by faith: but if *any man* draw back, my soul shall have no pleasure in him.

Hebrews 10:38

Now faith is the substance of things hoped for, the evidence of things not seen.

Hebrews 11:1

Through faith we understand that the worlds were framed by the word of God, so that things which are seen were not made of things which do appear.

Hebrews 11:3

By faith Abel offered unto God a more excellent sacrifice than Cain, by which he obtained witness that he was righteous, God testifying of his gifts: and by it he being dead yet speaketh.

Hebrews 11:4

By faith Enoch was translated that he should not see death; and was not found, because God had translated him: for before his translation he had this testimony, that he pleased God.

Hebrews 11:5

But without faith *it is* impossible to please *him:* for he that cometh to God must believe that he is, and *that* he is a rewarder of them that diligently seek him.

Hebrews 11:6

By faith Noah, being warned of God of things not seen as yet, moved with fear, prepared an ark to the saving of his house; by the which he condemned the world, and became heir of the righteousness which is by faith.

Hebrews 11:7

By faith Abraham, when he was called to go out into a place which he should after receive for an inheritance, obeyed; and he went out, not knowing whither he went. By faith he sojourned in the land of promise, as *in* a strange country, dwelling in tabernacles with Isaac and Jacob, the heirs with him of the same promise.

Hebrews 11:8–9

Through faith also Sarah herself received strength to conceive seed, and was delivered of a child when she was past age, because she judged him faithful who had promised.

Hebrews 11:11

By faith Abraham, when he was tried, offered up Isaac: and he that had received the promises offered up his only begotten *son.*

Hebrews 11:17

By faith Moses, when he was born, was hid three months of his parents, because they saw *he was* a proper child; and they were not afraid of the king's commandment.

Hebrews 11:23

By faith Moses, when he was come to years, refused to be called the son of Pharaoh's daughter; choosing rather to suffer affliction with the people of God, than to enjoy the pleasures of sin for a season; esteeming the reproach of Christ greater riches than the treasures in Egypt: for he had respect unto the recompence of the reward. By faith he forsook Egypt, not fearing the wrath of the king: for he endured, as seeing him who is invisible. Through faith he kept the passover, and the sprinkling of blood, lest he that destroyed the firstborn should touch them. By faith they passed through the Red sea as by dry *land:* which the Egyptians assaying to do were drowned.

Hebrews 11:24–29

By faith the walls of Jericho fell down, after they were compassed about seven days.

Hebrews 11:30

By faith the harlot Rahab perished not with them that believed not, when she had received the spies with peace.

Hebrews 11:31

Looking unto Jesus the author and finisher of *our* faith; who for the joy that was set before him endured the cross, despising the shame, and is set down at the right hand of the throne of God.

Hebrews 12:2

If any of you lack wisdom, let him ask of God, that giveth to all *men* liberally, and upbraideth not; and it shall be given him. But let him ask in faith, nothing wavering. For he that wavereth is like a wave of the sea driven with the wind and tossed.

James 1:5–6

Hearken, my beloved brethren, Hath not God chosen the poor of this world rich in faith, and heirs of the kingdom which he hath promised to them that love him?

James 2:5

What *doth it* profit, my brethren, though a man say he hath faith, and have not works? can faith save him?…Even so faith, if it hath not works, is dead, being alone.

James 2:14,17

For as the body without the spirit is dead, so faith without works is dead also.

James 2:26

And the prayer of faith shall save the sick, and the Lord shall raise him up; and if he hath committed sins, they shall be forgiven him.

James 5:15

That the trial of your faith, being much more precious than of gold that perisheth, though it be tried with fire, might be found unto praise and honour and glory at the appearing of Jesus Christ.

1 Peter 1:7

About the Author

For over four decades, Andrew Wommack has traveled America and the world teaching the truth of the Gospel. His profound revelation of the Word of God is taught with clarity and simplicity, emphasizing God's unconditional love and the balance between grace and faith. He reaches millions of people through the daily *Gospel Truth* radio and television programs, broadcast both domestically and internationally. He founded Charis Bible College in 1994 and has since established CBC extension schools in other major cities of America and around the world. Andrew has produced a library of teaching materials, available in print, audio, and visual formats. And, as it has been from the beginning, his ministry continues to distribute free audio materials to those who cannot afford them.

To contact Andrew Wommack, please write, e-mail, or call:

Andrew Wommack Ministries
P.O. Box 3333
Colorado Springs, CO 80934-3333
E-mail: awommack@aol.com
Helpline Phone (orders and prayer): 719-635-1111
Hours: 4:00 AM to 9:30 PM MST

Andrew Wommack Ministries of Europe

P.O. Box 4392

WS1 9AR Walsall

England

E-mail: enquiries@awme.net

U.K. Helpline Phone (orders and prayer):

011-44-192-247-3300

Hours: 5:30 AM to 4:00 PM GMT

Or visit him on the Web at: www.awmi.net

The Believer's Authority

The controversial subject of the authority of the believer in Christ is widely discussed in the Church today. Andrew Wommack brings a fresh perspective to this important spiritual truth that may challenge everything you've been taught including:

- If believers have been given authority, then when, how, and toward what should it be exercised? Don't assume the answer; discover the true battleground and learn how to recognize the real enemy.

- Most people believe God created our enemy, Satan, but did He? Understanding the answer will set you free to exercise your authority as a believer.

- Is spiritual warfare, as taught in many churches today, valid? Can believers use their authority to fight the devil and his demons in the air, or is the real battle in the mind? The answer is an important prerequisite to winning spiritual battles.

Digging into the scriptures, Andrew reveals the spiritual significance of your choices, words, and actions and how they affect your ability to stand against the attacks of Satan and to receive God's best. Discover the

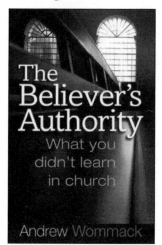

powerful truths behind true spiritual authority and begin seeing real results.

Item Code: 1045-C6-CD album
Item Code: 1045-D5-DVD album

ISBN: 1-57794-936-6 Paperback

Available at bookstores everywhere
or visit **www.harrisonhouse.com**

The War Is Over

Peace has been won. The longest conflict in history lasted 4,000 years and ended in a decisive victory nearly 2,000 years ago. Still, many have not yet heard the news and they continue to fight the battle—the battle of sin and judgment.

On the cross Jesus said, "It is finished," victory was declared, and reconciliation began. It was the victory promised when Jesus was born and the angels declared, "Glory to God in the highest, and on earth peace, good will toward men" (Luke 2:14). Is this saying Jesus came to create peace among men? If it is, then He has most certainly failed.

The peace He spoke of was not among men, but between God and man. Sin is no longer the issue; the price has been paid once and for all. God sent His only Son to bear our sin, becoming sin itself, and then judged Him without mercy for that sin. Was His sacrifice enough for you? Is God withholding His blessing because of your sin? If you die with an unconfessed sin, would you be lost? The answers contained in this book will release you from the condemnation of judgment and fear. It will free you to receive the promised blessings of God!

THE WAR IS OVER

God is Not
Mad, So Stop
Struggling With
Sin and Judgment

Andrew Wommack

Item Code: 1053-C 5-CD album
Item Code: 1053-D 6-DVD album

ISBN: 1-57794-935-8 Paperback

Available at bookstores everywhere
or visit **www.harrisonhouse.com**

Other Teachings by Andrew Wommack

Spirit, Soul, & Body

Understanding the relationship of your spirit, soul, and body is foundational to your Christian life. You will never truly know how much God loves you or believe what His Word says about you until you do. In this series, learn how they're related and how that knowledge will release the life of your spirit into your body and soul. It may even explain why many things are not working the way you had hoped.

Item Code: 318   Paperback
Item Code: 1027-C   4-CD album

The True Nature of God

Are you confused about the nature of God? Is He the God of judgment found in the Old Testament or the God of mercy and grace found in the New Testament? Andrew's revelation on this subject will set you free and give you a confidence in your relationship with God like never before. This is truly nearly-too-good-to-be-true news.

Item Code: 308   Paperback
Item Code: 1002-C   5-CD album

The Effects of Praise

Every Christian wants a stronger walk with the Lord. But how do you get there? Many don't know the true power of praise. It's essential. Listen as Andrew teaches biblical truths that will spark not only understanding but will help promote spiritual growth so you will experience victory.

Item Code: 309   Paperback
Item Code: 1004-C   3-CD album

God Wants You Well

Health is something everyone wants. Billions of dollars are spent each year trying to retain or restore health. So why does religion tell us that God uses sickness to teach us something? It even tries to make us believe that sickness is a blessing. That's just not true. God wants you well!

Item Code: 1036-C   4-CD album